A Collins English Course

Anthony Forrester ＊ *Alison Savage*

Course Consultant – Tony Duff

CollinsELT

A Division of HarperCollinsPublishers

CollinsELT
A division of HarperCollins Publishers
77–85 Fulham Palace Road
London W6 8JB

© Collins ELT 1991

First published 1991

10 9 8 7 6 5 4 3 2 1

Designed by Chi Leung.

Artwork by Andrew Aloof, John Batten, Kathy Baxendale, Peter Bull, Amy Burch, Tony Coles, Jerry Collins, Richard Deverall, Hardlines, Illustrated Arts, Susan Hunter, Frances Lloyd, David Parkins, David Simonds, Trevor Stanesby, Paul Sullivan, Clyde Pearson, Gillian Martin.

Set in 10/11pt Monotype Garamond ITC and composed on CollinsELT Electronic Text Management system using 3B2.
Printed in Italy by G. Canale & C.S.p.A

ISBN 0 00 370 473 4

This course is accompanied by a Teacher's Book ISBN 0 00 370 475 0, Practice Book ISBN 0 00 370 474 2 and a set of two cassettes ISBN 0 00 370 476 9.

Acknowledgements

Many people have contributed to this project, and the authors would particularly like to thank:

their families – Kate, Victoria, Jeremy, and Michael, Samia and Muna. Without their support and tolerance the writing task would have been immeasurably more difficult.

Collins ELT, particularly the editorial team, for their help and advice and their gentle chivvying, and Chi Leung for his designs and interesting ideas.

Tony Duff, of International House, for his comments and ideas as Course Consultant.

Martyn Ellis and Sarah Turnbull for their comments on the draft material.

Special acknowledgements to Beverley Costa and Martyn Ellis for their ideas and contributions to the course.

The publishers are grateful to the following for permission to reproduce material on the pages specified.

Texts and illustrations:
British Telecom Plc for extract from emergency services brochure, 53. Collins Travel and General Reference, 28; Collett, Dickenson, Pearce and Partners Ltd., British Sugar Plc, Tate & Lyle Plc for advertisement on sugar, 92; Collins Travel and General Reference for extracts from Collins Traveller Guide to London, 27; Longman Higher Education and Reference for maps from 'Peters Atlas of the World' (copyright Akademische Verlagsanstalt 1989. Used by permission of Longman Group UK Ltd. No reproduction may be made of or from this image), 29, 30; Trinidad and Tobago Tourist Office, 98; Which? Magazine for extracts from their feature 'Green Presents', 78.

Photographs
Ace Photo Agency, 11, 25, 28, 60 (3); Art Directors Photo Library, 84, 111, Anthony Blake, 91 (3), 89; Ardea London Ltd., Unit 18. The Bridgeman Art Library (copyright Harrogate Museums and Art Gallery), 33; Austin J Brown Aviation Picture Library, 4; Bubbles, 21 (3); Cadbury Ltd. External Services Departmetnt, 91; Cephas Picture Library, 4, 21, 41, 57, 75, 83; Bruce Coleman Ltd, 9, 28; The Environmental Picture Library, 67; Greg Evans Photo Library International, 28, 84; Tim Graham, 22; Sally & Richard Greenhill, 57; Susan Griggs Agency, 60; Pauline Hancock, 86; Robert Harding Picture Library, 4 (2), 11; John Harvey, 67; Ralf–finn Hestoft/Saba, 22; Holt Studios Ltd, 87; Hulton Picture Library, 87 (3); Hutchinson Library, 57; J Allan Cash Ltd, 9 (3), 11, 25 (2), 75 (2), 101; The Image Bank, 41 (6); 44, 70, 100; International House, 84; Life File Photo Library, 9, 57, 84, 67 (4), 75; Christine Osborne Pictures, 11; Pictures Colour Library, 11; Quadrant Picture Library, 84; Chris Shelton, 111; Spectrum Colour Library, 11, 25, 28; Tony Stone Worldwide, 99 (4); Syndication International Ltd, 25; The Telegraph Colour Library, 75; Viewfinder, 21; Visionbank/England Scene, 28, 57.

The publishers would also like to thank Dawn Aloof for taking photographs for the purpose of artists' reference, and Beaulieu and Longleat House for their help with material for page 112.

Note page 99 Figures for Germany do not include those relating to the former GDR, as statistics were not available at the time of going to press.

Contents

Map of the Book

Unit	Topics	Structures	Functions	Study skills

1	Meetings
	Introductions
	Learning
	English
		Revision of *Wh-* questions
		Revision of personal pronouns
		Revision of possessive
		  adjectives
		Revision of *have to*
			Greeting and introducing
			  people
			Exchanging personal
			  information
			Describing people
				Spelling
				Pronunciation

2	Airport
	information
	Accommo-
	dation
		Revision of *Wh-* questions
		Revision of instruction form
		Relative pronouns *which* and
		  who
		Revision of superlative
		shall
		Let's
			Making suggestions
			Understanding and giving
			  instructions
			Talking about accommodation
				Pronunciation: *wh-* questions

3	Visit to
	international
	conference
	centre
		Revision of prepositions of
		  place *opposite, next to,
		  between*
		Preposition of place *behind, in
		  front of*
		Prepositions of direction
		  *across, into, along, past,
		  through, over*
		Demonstrative pronouns *this,
		  that, these, those*
		Verbs + direct/indirect objects
			Asking for/giving directions
			Asking for/giving information
				Vocabulary: compound nouns

4	Youth Old age The future	Revision of *can/can't, has to/must* (not) adjective + *enough (to ...)* *too* + adjective (*to ...*) Revision of future (*going to*) Future with *will* *Will be able* *Could* (past of *can*)	Expressing obligation Predicting the future Talking about ability	Pronunciation: *will*
5	City Lights	REVISION OF UNITS 1 – 4		

6	Economic and
	social trends
		Quantifiers *all of, most of, a lot
		  of, some of, a little/few of,
		  not much/many of, none of*
		Revision of present continuous
			Analysing facts and figures
			Talking about present
			  developments/trends
				Pronunciation

7	Homes
	Housing
	Invitations
		Revision of *have got*
		Revision of *there is*
		There was/were/will be
		Reported speech (reporting
		  verb in present)
			Reporting messages and
			  instructions
			Inviting, accepting and
			  refusing invitations
			Making excuses
				Punctuation

8	Lifestyles	Simple present contrasted with
		  present continuous
		too much/many
		enough/not enough + noun
		Revision of adverbs of
		  frequency
			Talking about daily routine
			Talking about quantities
				Pronunciation: vowel sounds

9	Past events	Simple past contrasted with past continuous Conjunctions *and, but, so*	Discussing events Narrating stories	Spelling Syntax: conjunction
10	City Lights	REVISION OF UNITS 6 – 9		
11	Jobs Abilities Qualifications	Revision of *like/enjoy* +gerund *good at* + gerund Adverbs of manner	Expressing likes/dislikes Talking about qualities and talents	Vocabulary
12	Future plans Weather	Revision of future with *will* First conditional (*will*)	Making predictions about the future Giving advice	Syntax

Unit	Topics	Structures	Functions	Study skills
13	Hypothetical events	Second conditional (*would*)	Speculating about hypothetical situations Giving advice *If I were you . . .*	Stress and intonation
14	Protecting the environment Conservation	Commands — affirmative and negative forms Reported commands/requests *both . . . and* *either . . . or* Revision of possessive pronouns Revision of *too* + adjective, *(not)* adjective + *enough*	Reporting commands Giving advice Giving warnings Giving/asking for reasons	Vocabulary
15	City Lights	R E V I S I O N O F U N I T S 1 1 – 1 4		
16	Past and present	*Used to* – affirmative, negative and interrogative Revision of *ago* Partitives *cup/bottle/packet/loaf/litre/kilo of*	Talking about the past Making polite requests Persuading Talking about amounts	Punctuation
17	Facts and processes	Passive form – past and present Revision of *made of . . .*	Describing processes	Pronunciation: definite/indefinite articles
18	World geography Social statistics	Revision of comparative and superlative of adjectives Comparative of adjectives with *more . . . than*, *less . . . than*, *(not) as . . . as* Adverbs of degree	Comparing and contrasting Giving reasons	Vocabulary building
19	Holidays, parties Socialising	Question tags Determiners *too much/many, a little, a few* *so . . .* *Neither . . .*	Checking/confirming information Offering Accepting/refusing	Dictionary reference skills
20	City Lights	R E V I S I O N O F U N I T S 1 6 – 1 9		

Meetings and greetings

Look at the people in the pictures below.
Where do you think they are?

The people have just met.
What do you think they are saying?
Choose from these questions.

How old are you?
What do you do?
What's your name?
Where are you from?
What's your address?
What's your date of birth?
What's your telephone number?

What information do people want when
they ask questions like these?
Choose from this list.

JOB
DATE OF BIRTH
TELEPHONE NUMBER
ADDRESS
AGE
HOMETOWN
NAME

1

 Listen to the dialogues and match them with the pictures on page 1.

Now answer these questions about the dialogues.

Dialogue 1 Where are the men going?
Dialogue 2 What have the people got in common?
Dialogue 3 Where has the man just come from? Where is he going to stay?
Dialogue 4 What kind of party are they at?
Dialogue 5 What kind of company is it?

Listen again and check your answers.

2

 Listen to the dialogues again. What information do you hear in each dialogue?

Example
Dialogue 1   job, hometown

over to you

Ask questions and find out information about a partner. Write the information down.

Name ....
Age ....
Hometown ....
Job ....
Address ....

3

 Listen to these people talking at the party. Who is who?

Mary   secretary
Sally   student
Pedro   teacher

Listen again and put these greetings in the order you hear them.

Good evening. - Hello. - Pleased to meet you. -
How do you do? - Hi. -

Check your answers with a partner.

over to you

Now introduce yourself and your partner to other students in the class. Ask about the other students.

Hello, I'm ... .
This is ... .
He's/She's ... .
He's/She's from ... .
What about you?

4

Read this letter from Sally and answer the questions.

- Is she writing about old friends or new friends?
- Where is she?
- Who do you think Sally is writing to?

and I met some interesting people at the Browns' party recently. There's a really nice girl called Mary, from Cambridge. She's a teacher at the school where I work, so we always have a lot to talk about! Like me, she loves animals. She's got a dog and two cats! Mary introduced me to Pedro. He comes from Madrid and he's studying economics at a college here in Oxford. Pedro's living with the Browns. They're in the construction business and they've got a house with a wonderful swimming pool. Lucky Pedro! Through Pedro, I met Peter. He's in the construction business too. He's an engineer. He has a fabulous sports car and we've been on lots of trips around the country-side. His younger sister, Fiona, is really nice too. So, you see, I'm not lonely at all! You don't need to worry about me! I'm just fine

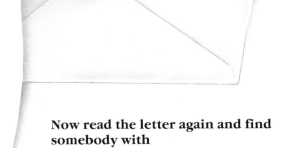

Now read the letter again and find somebody with

- a car
- a swimming pool
- a younger sister
- a teaching job
- pets at home.

Now make notes about the people in Sally's letter.

Example
Mary - teacher - comes from Cambridge - loves animals

5

Look at these personal pronouns and possessive adjectives and complete the table.

I	your	him	us	her	our	you
them	his	their	they	he	she
me	my	we	you	her

Now complete these sentences. Use words from your table.

1 ...... name is Pedro and ...... come from Madrid.
2 Pedro's brother's name is José and ......'s an engineer.
3 Mary is a teacher and ...... comes from Sydney, Australia.
4 The Browns live in Oxford. ....'re in the construction business and ...... house has a wonderful swimming pool.
5 Peter's got a younger sister. ...... name is Fiona and ......'s a nurse.

Look at the clothes below. Do you recognise them?

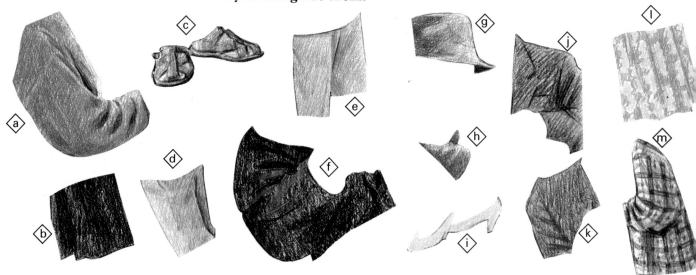

Name them and say what colour they are. Choose from these words.

red   sandals   scarf   jumper   jeans   green   trousers   brown   skirt

t-shirt   trainers   jacket   shoes   yellow   black   dress   shirt   hat

suit   white   orange   blouse

Now look back at page 1. Who is wearing them?

Example   Mary's wearing the red blouse.

Look around the class and make a list of five items of clothing.

Example
a red shirt

Describe a student by his/her clothes. Ask the others to guess who it is.

Example
You	This person's wearing a red shirt.
Class	Is it Frank?
You	No, it isn't.
Class	Is it ... ?

7

Look at these pictures of different people in different jobs.

- What do they do?
- Where do they work?
- How do they use English in their jobs? Do they have to speak, write, read or listen?

🖭 **Now listen to the interviews with the people and check your answers. Make notes and then write about each person.**

In groups, discuss how you have to use English in your jobs.

Example
I'm an air hostess. I have to listen to English and I have to speak English to the passengers.

Look at these contexts for English and match them with the pictures.

conversations
newspapers and magazines
film
radio
letters
songs
messages

Now put them into these four groups.

Listening 👂	Speaking 👄	Reading 📖	Writing ✒
conversations	conversations		

For what purposes do you need English?

Example
I need English to write letters.

Find out why other students in your class need English and write sentences.

Example
Antonio needs English to listen to the radio and to read books.

Make a list of other activities for which you need English. Put them under the four headings.

How many words from this unit can you put into these groups? Complete the lists.

Introductions	Greetings	Clothes	Jobs
this is...	hello	jacket	air hostess

a Listen to the alphabet and underline the letters which are pronounced wrongly.

A B C D E F G H I J
K L M N O P Q R S T
U V W X Y Z

Say the alphabet to a partner correctly, then listen to the tape and check.

b Spell this word to your partner.
conversation

Complete these words from the unit and then spell them to your partner.

_ _ ll _	_ am _	a _ d _ _ ss
l _ s _ e _ i _ g	_ r _ t _ n _	_ e _ d _ _ g
sp _ _ k _ n _	_ ki _ t	_ h _ es

Work together and put the words in alphabetical order.
Listen to the tape and check your answers.

Grammar and Language

1 Greetings

You can use these expressions when you meet people.

> Hi.
> Hello.
> How do you do?
> Pleased to meet you.
> Good morning/afternoon/evening.

2 Introductions

You can use these expressions to introduce yourself and other people.

Yourself			Other people	
I'm My name's	Sam.		This is Meet	Sally.

3 Personal pronouns and possessive adjectives

You can use a personal pronoun to replace a name or noun when it is clear who you are referring to.

You can use a possessive adjective to show possession/connection when it is clear who you are referring to.

Subject pronouns		Object pronouns		Possessive adjectives	
Singular	Plural	Singular	Plural	Singular	Plural
I	we	me	us	my	our
you	you	you	you	your	your
he she it	they	him her it	them	his her its	their

A subject pronoun represents the subject of the clause.
(*Mary*'s a teacher.) **She** teaches in Oxford.

An object pronoun represents the object of the clause.
(I was a student at *Mary*'s school.) I met **her** there.

You can use a possessive adjective to show who something belongs to.
(Hello. Pleased to meet *you*.) What's **your** name?

You can also use a possessive adjective to show that people are connected.
(Hello, *Mary*.) Who is **your** friend?
(I met *Peter*.) **His** younger sister is really nice.

Arrivals and departures

Look at the signs in the pictures.
Where do you find signs like these?

(a)

Passport control

(b)

Check-in

(c) **Departures**

Customs

(d)

(e)

Arrivals

Baggage reclaim

Meeting point

(f)

(g)

Imagine that you have just arrived at an airport.
Work with a partner and decide which signs to follow and in what order.

2

1

Look at this picture.

- Who are the people?
- What do you think is happening?

Information

Listen to the tape and complete the directions.

Follow the signs to .... First you have to show your ...... to the immigration officer at .... Then you can collect your ...... in the ...... hall. After that, you have to go through .... Maybe the ...... officer will want to ...... your ...... and your ....

Which airport signs do you have to follow when you <u>leave</u> a country? Write instructions for somebody who does not know.

2

Find these people in the pictures on page 7.

porter
customs officer
ground hostess
immigration officer

Answer these questions.

1 Who checks your passport?
2 Who helps you with your luggage?
3 Who checks your ticket and gives you your seat number?
4 Who checks your luggage?

Describe what the people do.

Example
The immigration officer is the person who checks your passport.

Now make sentences about the other people in the picture on page 7.

3

**Look at the passengers who have just arrived.
What can you say about them?
Where do you think they want to go now?**

4

Look back at the pictures in exercise 3.
Listen to the tape. Decide who is speaking in each dialogue and which signs they are going to follow.

Listen again. Which of these suggestions can you hear in which dialogue?

Shall we ... ?   Let's ...   Why don't we ... ?   Why don't you ... ?

Work in pairs.

Ⓐ **Look at page 114.**

Ⓑ **Listen to your partner's problems and make suggestions, using the expressions above.**

Example

Ⓐ I've lost my suitcase.

Ⓑ Let's tell a ground hostess.

5

Read these advertisements.

- What are they for?
- Where can you find advertisements like these?
- Are any suitable for the passengers?

Read the advertisements carefully again and answer these questions.

1 Which type of accommodation do you think is the most expensive, and which is the cheapest?
2 Which do you think is the noisiest and why?
3 In which types of accommodation can people do their own cooking?
4 Which type of accommodation would you like and why?

Small country cottage to let for one year. Ideal for small family. Reasonable rent. Ring 2503 and ask for Bill.

HOTEL SUPERIOR New luxury hotel. Near airport. Ideal for business travellers. Conference facilities available. Swimming pool, sauna. Tel.: 2345.

FAIRWAY HOTEL Small, comfortable hotel. Peaceful situation in quiet suburb. Ideal for short-stay guests who want peace and quiet. Tel.: 27923.

Room in family home to let for one year. Fully furnished. Own bathroom and cooking facilities. Would suit student. Ring 512249.

Seaside bungalow for holiday let. Would suit couple or family. Reasonable prices. For further information, ring 7771.

6

 Listen to two passengers asking about accommodation and complete the table using √ (=yes) or x (= no).

	short stay	long stay	single room	double room	own bathroom	own cooking	car park
Student							
Business-woman							

Write about the two people. Consider these points as you write.

- How long do they want to stay?
- Do they want a single room/double room?
- Do they want their own bathroom?
- Do they want to do their own cooking?
- Do they need a car park?

Now look at the advertisements on page 9 again and find the best accommodation for each person.

7

You (A) have just arrived at the airport and your partner (B) is the information officer . Work with your partner and find suitable accommodation for yourself. This chart will help you.

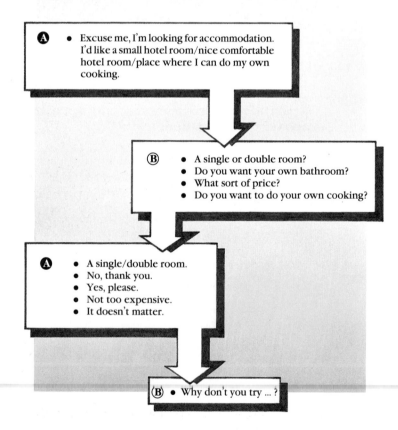

A
- Excuse me, I'm looking for accommodation. I'd like a small hotel room/nice comfortable hotel room/place where I can do my own cooking.

B
- A single or double room?
- Do you want your own bathroom?
- What sort of price?
- Do you want to do your own cooking?

A
- A single/double room.
- No, thank you.
- Yes, please.
- Not too expensive.
- It doesn't matter.

B • Why don't you try ... ?

Study points

a Listen and repeat these question words.

which   who   what   why   where   when

In which word is the *wh* sound different? In what way is it different?

b Each word below rhymes with one of the words above. Can you match them?

too   by   pot   wear   switch   ten

Listen and check.

Find more words which rhyme with the words above.

Now ask B (the information officer) to write a telex or fax to book your accommodation. Check that the details are right.

8

Look at the rooms below and decide which

- is the most expensive/cheapest.
- is the smallest.
- is/are for two people.
- is the biggest.

**Look at the rooms very carefully again.
Find the room/s which**

- has/have a balcony
- overlook/s the sea
- has/have a television.

Which room do you like best? What do you like about it? Which room don't you like? Tell a partner.

Example
I like the room which overlooks the sea.
I don't like the room which .....

9

**Complete these advertisements.
Use *who* or *which*.**

This is a splendid, historical city ...... is sometimes known as 'The Athens of the North'. For people ...... want to relax, enjoy history and culture and experience true Scottish hospitality, it is the ideal place for a perfect holiday.

This is a delightful northern city ...... is famous for its canals. People ...... visit it regularly call it 'The Venice of the North'.

This island is not for the visitor ...... is looking for constant sunshine on holiday. It is an island ...... is often called 'The Emerald Isle' and is both beautiful and mysterious.

Decide where these places are. Why do you think they have the special names?

over to you

**Write about two cities or places which you know.
Give your descriptions to your partner.
Your partner must guess what and where they are.**

Grammar and Language

1 *Wh*-questions

When you ask a question beginning with a wh-word or how, you expect the answer to give you information. You do not expect simply 'yes' or 'no' as an answer.

Questions   Answers

What sort of price?	$\longrightarrow$	Not too expensive.
Why is this room noisy?	$\longrightarrow$	Because it's near the airport.
Where do you find these signs?	$\longrightarrow$	In an airport.
When are we going to see her?	$\longrightarrow$	Right now.
Who checks your passport?	$\longrightarrow$	The immigration officer.
Which room do you like best?	$\longrightarrow$	The one overlooking the sea.
How long do you want to stay?	$\longrightarrow$	Two months.

2 Relative pronouns *who* and *which*

Relative pronouns join clauses together.

a The relative pronoun *who* refers back to a person/people.

He is the *person*	**who**	checks your passport.
It is ideal for *people*		want to relax.

b The relative pronoun *which* refers back to a thing/things.

It is a *place*	**which**	is famous for its canals.
There are *two rooms*		have a balcony.

3 Suggestions

You can use these expressions to make suggestions.

Shall we **Why don't we** **Why don't you**	have a coffee?
Let's	have a coffee.

4 *own*

You can use *own* which you want to emphasise that something belongs to/is connected with a particular person or thing You can use *own* after possessive adjectives and nouns with *'s*.

Your The guest's The room's	**own**	bathroom.

A city under one roof

What kind of building is this? Who are the people? Describe them.

Describe where each person is. Use these prepositions.

next to	in front of	behind	between	opposite

1

Here is a list of places in the building. Does it give you any more ideas about the kind of building?

> restaurant   post office   information desk
> hairdresser's   bank   souvenir shop
> sports centre   telephones   car park
> conference centre   lifts   taxi rank
> newsagent's

Now listen to the announcement on the tape. Were you right?

Where do you think the people in the main picture are going? Work with a partner and compare your ideas.

2

Make a list of questions you can use to ask for directions. Now look at the four people standing at the information desk and decide:

- where they want to go.
- what questions they are going to ask.

Now listen and check your answers. Make a note of the questions they ask.

Listen again and make notes about the directions that are given. These words will help you.

> along   across   into   over   through   past

Compare your notes with a partner's.

3

Listen to the tape once again. This time, look at the diagram and follow the directions.

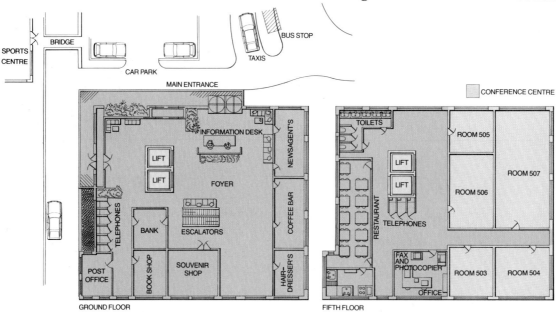

GROUND FLOOR

FIFTH FLOOR

Here is one of the dialogues from the tape. Try to complete it. Refer to the diagram to help you.

Visitor	Good morning.
Receptionist	Good morning, Madam. Can I help you?
Visitor	Oh, yes. Thank you. How .... to the conference centre, please? I've got a meeting in room 506.
Receptionist	No problem. The conference centre is .... floor. Just .... up to the ...... floor and you'll find room 506 ...... the lift.
Visitor	Thank you very much.

Look at these situations. Decide where you need to go and use the diagram to find the way.

- You want to buy some presents.
- You want to send a fax.
- You want to go into town.
- You want to change some traveller's cheques.

Work with a partner. Ask for and give directions.

Example

Ⓐ Excuse me, how do I get to the tennis courts, please?

Ⓑ You just walk out through the main doors, across the car park, over the bridge and into the sports centre.

Choose two other places on the diagram and ask for directions.

4

Someone is coming to meet you at the international centre. Leave this person a note explaining where you are going to be and giving directions.

Example

Take the lift up to the fifth floor. Come out of the lift. Turn right, then right again. Go past the telephones and the restaurant is right in front of you.

5

Look at the two pictures below. Which of these words do you associate with each of the pictures?

> luxurious style cool air-conditioned market
> modern crowded jewellery hot fashions traditional

Now look at the two texts. What kinds of texts are they? Choose from these answers.

a holiday brochure   b publicity information   c formal letter
d informal letter   e newspaper report

Read the texts and answer the questions.

Dear Rita and Tom,

Hope you're well and not working too hard! It's extremely hot here, but we're really enjoying it. The conference is going well, and we're staying in a luxurious modern hotel, the Shilton International. It's got everything you need, including its own shopping plaza!

We had a little free time yesterday and we went to the local 'souk' - that's Arabic for 'market'. It was so crowded and hot - no air-conditioning there! But I really loved it. It was fascinating to see all the things for sale - traditional rugs and carpets, clothes and jewellery. Everything under the sun!

And talking of jewellery, we wanted to bring Carla a traditional souvenir and so we bought her a lovely pair of gold earrings there. It was very difficult to decide, because the man showed us so many different earrings. He also gave us a beautifully decorated box for the earrings. So Carla should be happy. But what on earth can we get Steve?

The Shilton International Centre Welcomes You

The management and staff would like to welcome you to the Shilton International Centre. We hope you will enjoy your stay and take advantage of the wide range of facilities available.

From your comfortable rooms on the first floor, you have easy access to the rest of the complex. You can dine in style in our first-class restaurant on the fifth floor.

An important meeting? We have a superb, well-equipped conference centre also on the fifth floor.

Shop in comfort in the Shilton International's air-conditioned basement shopping plaza where you'll find everything from the latest Paris fashions to local souvenirs.

All this and much more at the Shilton International.

1 What is the Arabic word for 'market'?
2 Is it hot in the shopping plaza?
3 Where can you buy traditional things to wear?
4 Which would you prefer, the modern shopping plaza or the souk? Why?
5 Were you right about the words above (luxurious, style etc)?

6

Look back at the texts in exercise 5 and find these nouns.

| rooms   restaurant   conference centre   hotel   clothes   box   earrings |

Which adjectives are used to describe them?

Example
comfortable rooms

7

Find out how these sentences are expressed in the letter. Notice the differences.

1 He also gave a beautifully decorated box to us.
2 The man showed so many different earrings to us.
3 We wanted to bring a traditional souvenir for Carla.
4 We bought a lovely pair of gold earrings for her.
5 What on earth can we get for Steve?

Now rewrite the sentences below so that they do not contain *to* or *for*.

Example
We bought a ring for Alice.
We bought Alice a ring.

1 We're sending the ring to Alice.
2 Shall we bring a souvenir for you, too?
3 We've written a letter to Jo, too.
4 We're giving a necklace to Maggie and a watch to Martin.
5 We'll show all the presents to you at the weekend.
6 What can we buy for Steve?

Study points

A compound is a word formed from two or more words.

Example
A bottle which holds milk is a *milk bottle*.

How many compounds can you make from this list?

living   park   room   car   conference
pool   office   conditioning   air   post
plaza   shopping   court   tennis
centre   swimming

Now find the compounds for the following definitions.

1 The place where you catch a bus.
2 A person who works in a bank.
3 A room where you eat.
4 A drink made form oranges.
5 A person who works in a shop.

Find three more compounds and write definitions.
Ask a partner to guess the compounds.

8

Look at the pictures and then complete the table.

9

Work with a partner. Where do you think these objects come from, the souk or the Shilton International? Use the table to help you.

| I think | this
that
these
those | ... | is from
are from | ..., but | this
that
these
those | one is from
ones are from | ... |

10

Work with a partner. Find out more about the Shilton International.

Ⓐ Look at page 114.

Ⓑ Read the texts and complete the chart below.

Then ask your partner questions to find out the missing information.

Example
Where's the post office?
Can you tell me the opening hours of the post office?

	Location	Opening hours	Telephone numbers
post office			
bank			
bookshop			
cafeteria			
travel agent's			
newsagent's			

over to you

Write a short paragraph about banks and post offices in your country.

- What are their opening times?
- What facilities do they offer?

Compare notes with your partner.

SHOPPING AT THE SHILTON

Bank

The Shilton Bank is on the ground floor, with full banking facilities, including a fast foreign exchange service. The bank is open from 9.00 - 12.00 and 13.30 - 17.00, Monday - Friday. Tel.: 2002318.

Cafeteria

You'll find our international cafeteria, serving light meals and drinks, in the basement. This delightful eating place is open daily for breakfast at 7 a.m. and closes at 8 p.m. Reserve a table by calling: 2003997.

Travel agent's

Make use of this excellent service located on the first floor. We are open from 9.00 - 17.30, every day except Sunday. If you have any questions, just call us on 2009337. We'll be happy to help.

Grammar and Language

1 Prepositions of place and direction

Prepositions are words that show a relationship between people, objects or events. Some of the most common refer to place and direction.

a You can use prepositions of place to describe where someone/something is in relation to someone/something else.

The swimming pool is The tourists are waiting	**opposite** **in** **next to** **near** **in front of** **behind**	the hotel.
The telephone is	**on**	the desk.
Room 503 is	**between**	the office and room 504.

b You can use prepositions of direction to give directions or describe routes. You use them with verbs of movement.

	along **across**	the road.
Go	**into** **past**	the hotel.
	through	the doors.
	over	the bridge.

2 Asking for directions

You can use this expression to ask for directions.

How do I / we get to the sports centre?

3 Verbs with direct and indirect and indirect object

Certain verbs can take a direct object followed by a prepositional phrase.

We	**wrote/sent/gave/showed** **brought/bought/got**	**a card**	*to* *for*	*Carla.* *her.*

Instead of using a prepositional phrase, you can use an indirect object followed by the direct objec

We	**wrote/sent/gave/showed** **brought/bought/got**	*Carla* *her*	a card.

4 Demonstrative adjectives *this, that, these, those*

You can use the demonstrative adjectives *this* and *these* to describe people/things that are close to you (here), and *that* and *those* for things that are at some distance (there).

Singular

This	key	here?
That	one	there?

Plural

These	keys	here?
Those	ones	there?

Growing older

Which of these words best describe the people in the pictures?

old young teenager adult baby middle-aged oldest youngest

**What can you say about each person? Use *can't* or *has to* in your sentences.
Use these words to help you.**

chew crawl go to school run see speak walk work

Example
The baby is the youngest. He can't walk. He has to crawl.

1

Look at the list of expressions below.
Which ones do you associate with the old
man/the young girl? Make two lists.

> glasses   exams   bad health   poor eyesight
> homework   walking stick   discos

Now listen to the tape.

- Who is talking?
- Were your associations correct?

**Listen again and complete the sentences
below.**

1   You ...... stay up late.
2   I ...... go to discos.
3   I ...... smoke.
4   I ...... use a walking stick.

**Now answer these questions about the girl
and the old man.**

1   Why can't she stay up late?
2   Why can't the girl go to discos?
3   Why mustn't the old man smoke?
4   Why does he have to use a walking stick?

2

**What do the girl's parents say to her?
Choose a, b or c.**

a   She can't go to discos. She's too old.
b   She can't go to discos. She's too young.
c   She can't go to discos. She's too small.

**Now look at this sentence.
Match it with a, b or c above.**

She's too young to go to discos.

**Combine the sentences below in the
same way.**

1   He can't stay up late. He's always too tired.
2   The baby can't talk. He's too young.
3   She can't afford a new coat. She's too poor.
4   She can't run upstairs. She's too weak.

Now look at this sentence.

She's not old enough to go to discos.

**Match it with a, b or c above.
Now rewrite your sentences using
*not ... enough to ...***

3

Look at the pictures and make a sentence
for each one, using these adjectives.

> unfit/fit   rich/poor   tall/short   fast/slow
> strong/weak   old/young

Example
3   He's old enough to drive a car.

over to you

**What about you? Make true sentences
about yourself using the pictures.
Write them down.**

Example
I'm old enough to drive a car./ I'm too young to
drive a car.

Ask your partner questions.

4

Listen to a conversation between the schoolgirl and her teacher and put sentences a-h in the right order.

a   Perhaps I'll stay on at school.
b   What are you going to do?
c   You're going to leave school soon.
d   I think that will be very useful, Jenny.
e   You won't get a good job without qualifications.
f   I suppose I'll just get a job.
g   And when will you be sixteen?
h   Are you going to take any exams before you leave?

Now choose the sentences which refer to future plans.

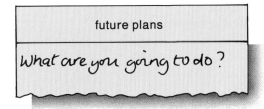

future plans

What are you going to do?

Listen to the tape again and correct these statements.

1   Jenny will get a good job without qualifications.
2   Qualifications won't help her to get a good job.
3   Jenny won't be 16 next month.
4   Jenny's teacher doesn't think good qualifications will help her.
5   Jenny won't take any exams.

5

Look at the photos. What are the children doing?

James

Susan

Tony

Sara

Martin and Daniel

Discuss with a partner what you think they will do or be when they grow up.

Example
Ⓐ What do you think Sara will do?
Ⓑ I think she'll be a teacher or a .... What do you think?

Write a sentence about each child.

**Look at the photo of these two young boys.
Do you recognise them?**

**Listen to 'royal observer', Kenneth Bennet,
talking about their future.
Choose the best title for the interview.**

a   Royal Family Life   c   Social Circles
b   A Royal Education   d   Royal Fashion

**Did the other students agree?
Explain why you chose your title.
Listen again and complete these sentences.**

1   They are naturally..... famous ..... to an ordinary school.
2   They will .... socialise with the right people.
3   Their father .... visit some of his friends.
4   No, they're ..... old .... go away yet.

**Now put these words in the right order
to make two of the interviewer's questions.**

1 live/home/will/they/at/?
2 they/Gordonstoun/will/go/to/?

over to you

Ⓐ **Imagine that you are a famous young person.**
Ⓑ **You are the interviewer. Ask about your
partner's future.**

**Before you read the text, look at these statements. Which do you think
are true and which are false?**

● People do not want to grow old.
● People have found ways of making themselves look younger.
● Special treatment can help people to play tennis.

Now read the text. Where you see a box, try to answer the question/questions.

Money can buy you youth!

People live longer nowadays than ever before. Take Britain,
for example. By the year 2020, there will probably be about 13 million
people over the age of 60.

1   How will this affect hospitals, doctors and nurses? What about housing?

In the past, people could not be as active and independent as they
can be today. Life was much more difficult in days gone by.
But one thing hasn't changed at all ... people are always trying to
make themselves look younger!

2   Can you think of some things which help people to look younger?

So nowadays people can overcome wrinkles, baldness and grey hair to some extent. Recently,
American doctors have developed a 'youth drug' treatment which makes people look younger and feel
stronger. Twenty-one men between the ages of 61 and 81 have recently tested the treatment for six months.
Before the treatment, some of the men could not walk properly. They felt weak and had no energy.

3   What do you think the men can do now after the treatment?

The doctors think that, because of this drug, more and more old people will be able to enjoy
a healthier life in future. Unfortunately, however, there is one big problem. When the treatment
is generally available, it will cost about $14,000 a year. And who will be able to afford that?

**Look at the text and your answer to question 2
again and complete this information.**

Before	Now
The men couldn't...	Now they can ....

Read the last paragraph of the text again

● How will the drug help people in the future?
● What will the main problem be?

8

Look carefully at these facts about two old people. They are going to take the 'youth drug'.

M Carter
Problems
wrinkles,
bad eyesight,
weak legs.

T Warner
Problems
too thin,
walking
difficulties,
general
weakness.

- Why do you think they are going to take the drug?
- What are their problems now? What can't they do?
- How will they change after the treatment?
- What will they be able to do?

In groups, discuss whether you think the drug is a good thing.

Study points

a **Listen to the sentences on tape. What do you hear?**
1 he'll *or* he
2 I'll *or* I
3 we'll *or* we
4 they'll *or* they
5 you'll *or* you

b **Now do the same for these sentences.**
1 they won't *or* they want
2 I won't *or* I want
3 we won't *or* we want
4 I won't *or* I want
5 you won't *or* you want

9

Work in groups and discuss what you think life will be like in the next century.

- What will people eat?
- What kind of clothes will people wear?
- How many hours a week will people work?
- How will people travel?
- Where will people spend their holidays?

Compare your ideas with another groups'.

Grammar and Language

1 *too* + adjective (*to ...*)/ *(not)* adjective + *enough* (*to ...*)

You can use *too* + adjective and *(not) adjective* + *enough* to help explain why something is impossible/possible.

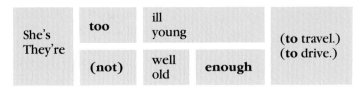

| She's They're | **too** | ill young | | (**to travel.**) (**to drive.**) |
| | (**not**) | well old | **enough** | |

2 *can:* **permission**

You can use *can/can't* to ask for/give/refuse permission.

| **Can** I go to the disco? | You **can't** go to the disco. |

3 **Future with** *will*

a You can use *will/will not* + infinitive to talk about events at some time in the future.
In spoken English, you usually shorten *will* to *'ll* (in statements) and *will not* to *won't*.

| Which school **will** they go to? | They'**ll**/They **won't** go to an ordinary school. |

b You can use the future with *will* after expressions like *perhaps, maybe, I think, I suppose, I hope.*

4 *could / be able to*

a You can use *could/couldn't* + infinitive to talk about ability/permission in the past. You can think of *could* as the past form of *can.*

| Last year, they **could/couldn't** drive. |

b You can use *will/won't be able to* + infinitive to talk about ability/permission in the future. You can think of *will be able to* as the future form of *can.*

| Very soon, they'**ll**/they **won't be able to** drive. |

Getting about

**Look at this month's edition of *City Lights*. What is the special feature?
Who is the reporter? Which country is featured in the travel section?**

City Lights
Can you get around the UK?
Plan your own week-end in London
How well do you know London?

City Lights

Contents

SPECIAL FEATURE

10 The Travel Business - Behind the Scenes.
Susie Harper writes about her experiences while travelling and staying in hotels.

REPORT

23 A Night in Casualty
Doug Young observes the work of doctors and nurses in the emergency ward of a busy city hospital.

31 Paul Newman - The Good Guy
Exclusive interview with Paul Newman.

REVIEW

2 Film and TV
The best of the latest films.

FASHION

47 Night Owl
A look at the latest fashions in evening wear.

FOOD AND DRINK

63 Who Needs Meat?
A guide to the best vegetarian restaurants in the country.

TRAVEL

70 Can you get around the UK?
An essential guide for tourists coming to the UK.

81 How well do you know London?
We give you a guided tour of London.

5

What other articles are in this month's magazine?

1

Susie went to Spain to research her report. Listen to these four short dialogues on her trip and match each dialogue with a picture.

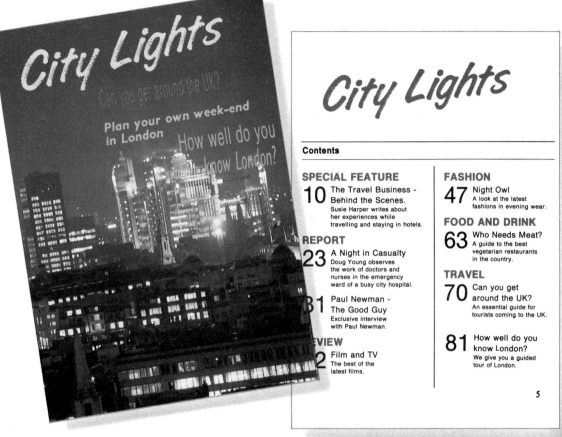

Travel agent's open 10 a.m. - 6 p.m. ⓐ

Chemist - open all day ⓑ

Bank ⓒ open 9.00 a.m - 12.00 p.m. 2.00 p.m. - 5.00 p.m.

Now act out the dialogues with a partner using the other pictures as prompts.

2

At one hotel, Susie interviewed the receptionist about the types of questions and problems the guests have. Make a list of the questions or problems you think they may have.

Now work with a partner. One of you is the receptionist, the other is the guest. Imagine you are in these situations. What do you say?

- The guest wants to know the cost of a single room.
- The guest wants directions to the nearest bank.
- The receptionist suggests a taxi for a guest who is in a hurry.
- The guest wants to know the opening times for the swimming pool.
- The guest asks the receptionist to give his/her wife/husband a message.
- The guest wants to know about meal times.

3

The magazine editor is correcting some sentences from Susie's article. Choose the correct word or words for each sentence.

1 A bus to the city centre (leaves/leave) from the airport every 20 minutes.
2 The hotel (have got/has got) 75 rooms.
3 (These/Those) bungalows under the trees over there were built last year.
4 If you stay in a bungalow, you can cook your (own/self) meals.
5 (This/That) is the new swimming pool here.
6 Children under five are (too/very) young to go in the swimming pool on their own.
7 The hotel is only 20 minutes' drive from a large town (who/which) is famous for its restaurants.
8 I (couldn't /couldn't to) check all the hotel's facilities.
9 I didn't get to the hotel early (enough/too) to have lunch.
10 The receptionist gave (to me/me) a nice room overlooking the sea.

4

Now the editor wants to rewrite some of the sentences in the story. Complete the new sentences.

Example
It is a busy place. It has an international atmosphere.
It is a busy place which has an international atmosphere.

1 There are a lot of good facilities in the hotel.
   The hotel ...
2 No smoking in the hotel.
   You mustn't ...
3 It is a hot country. It is popular with tourists.
   It is a hot country ...... is popular with tourists.
4 On the last day of my visit it rained, so windsurfing was impossible.
   On the last day of my visit it rained, so I ...
5 The receptionist gave some information about markets to me.
   The receptionist gave ...... some information about markets.

Look at these words.
tourist   hostel   expensive   capital
travel agent's

Match the words with their dictionary definitions.

▬▬ a house where people can stay cheaply for a short time, usually owned by a local government authority or charity.

▬▬ a business which makes arrangements for people's holidays and journeys.

▬▬ the city or town where a country's government or parliament is.

▬▬ a person who visits places for pleasure and interest.

▬▬ costing a lot of money.

Now put them in alphabetical order.

5

Susie recorded some typical conversations between the receptionist and hotel guests. Listen to one guest, Mrs Kennedy, who has lost her purse. Which picture matches Mrs Kennedy's description of her purse?

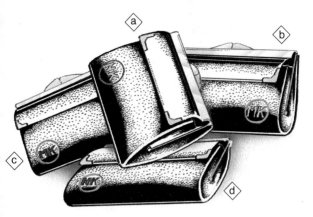

Listen to the conversation again and complete these sentences.

1 I'm sure .... find it somewhere.
2 I was sitting over there, ... that palm tree.
3 I'm sure .... do something.
4 Only the waiter .... was serving breakfast.
5 .... ask the manager to come down.

Mrs Kennedy phoned her husband and told him the story. He sent her some money at once. She wanted to send him a telegram which she wrote out...

> THANK YOU CHEQUE STOP POLICE TOMORROW STOP THINK WAITER STOLE PURSE STOP HOME ON THURSDAY STOP PLANE ARRIVES 5·15 PM STOP CATCH TRAIN AT AIRPORT STOP PLEASE MEET ME STOP

but she sent a letter instead.

> Dear Jim,
> Thank you for the cheque. I'm going to see the police tomorrow because I think the waiter stole my purse. I hope the police will arrest him. I'm going to come home on Thursday. The plane arrives at 5·15 pm. I'll catch the train from the airport. Will you be able to meet me at the station at 5·15 p.m?
> See you soon

Look at this telegram written by another guest who lost his passport and ticket. Can you rewrite it as a letter?

> LOST PASSPORT AND TICKET STOP POLICE
> THINK STOLEN STOP EMBASSY TOMORROW STOP
> HOME FRIDAY STOP PLANE LANDS 19.25 STOP
> MEET ME AT AIRPORT? STOP

6

Work in pairs. **Ⓐ** Look at page 114.
Ⓑ Look at the information from *City Lights* about visiting the UK. Then answer your partner's questions.

Passports and Customs A valid passport is required to enter Britain. Citizens of the USA, Commonwealth, European and South American countries do not require a visa. Visitors are limited to a stay of six months. Those wishing to stay longer should contact the Home Office, 50 Queen Anne Gate, SW1. Tel: 071 213 3000.

Bicycle and Motorbike Hire An ideal way of seeing London despite the heavy traffic. To hire one you will require a clean driving licence. Rates per day: mopeds from £10.95; motorcycles from £19.95; bicycles from £3.00 - £4.00. There are also reduced weekly rates.

Accommodation As you would expect, accommodation is most expensive in the west and south west of the city where many of the top quality hotels are located. More modest, but comfortable, hotels can be found around Victoria, Kensington and Bayswater. Reservations in advance are essential for the high season (usually May to September).

Traveller's Cheques and Credit Cards Sterling traveller's cheques are accepted in most major stores, but they usually charge a commission. You will get a better rate of exchange at banks. Remember to take your passport as proof of identity when changing money. The bureaux de change in the major railway stations are open late. Beware of the high commission charged by some of the bureaux de change - look for an LTB registered sign and ask the rate before you change any money. Credit cards are widely accepted.

Banks Banks are open 09.30 - 15.30 Mon. - Fri. (15.00 in the city) and are closed Sat., Sun. and public holidays. Some West End branches open late Thurs. (until 18.00 or 20.00) and Saturday morning (09.30 - 12.30). Heathrow and Gatwick (see Airports) have 24-hour banking and money changing facilities.

Ask your partner the following questions.

1 Can I get a taxi from the airport?
2 What do I need to drive my car in the UK?
3 Can I take cigarettes into the UK?
4 What's the electricity voltage?
5 How many pence are there in a £ (pound sterling)?

Now work together to complete these sentences.

1 You must be over ...... to hire a motor-bike.
2 You must drive on the ...... in Britain.
3 Visitors can stay for ...... months.
4 You have to show your ...... when you enter Britain.
5 Banks close at ...... and are not open on ....
6 You have to ...... a room in London hotels.
7 Electric plugs in the UK have ...... pins.
8 You can travel from the airport by ....

Look at these pictures of famous places. Find them on the map.

Choose the right words from the list below to complete this guided tour of central London.

1 in on at for
2 right left up on
3 see look get take
4 north south east top
5 house live lives goes
6 left middle right under
7 walk pass look get
8 at for to by
9 down up past through

Begin ...(1)... Charing Cross Station. Turn ...(2)... down the Strand and then left again to the top of Whitehall. From here you can look across Trafalgar Square and ...(3)... Nelson's Column, and the pigeons, lions and fountains. On the ...(4)... side of the square is the National Gallery, a famous art museum. Go along Whitehall. You will pass government ministries, and on the right you will see Downing Street, where the Prime Minister ...(5)... . When you get to Parliament Square, you will see Big Ben and the Houses of Parliament on your ...(6)... . Turn right into Broad Sanctuary and you will ...(7)... Westminster Abbey, the most famous church in London. Now turn right again into Storey's Gate and continue ...(8)... the entrance to St James's Park. Walk ...(9)... the park, across the bridge until you get to Buckingham Palace, the home of the Royal Family. Next, walk up Constitution Hill until you reach Hyde Park Corner.

Work in groups or pairs and plan your own holiday. Decide where you want to go ... to a city, the country or the coast. Think about the following things.

- where you are going to stay... in a hotel or in self-catering accommodation
- what you want to see/visit
- how long you are going to stay
- how you will get there.

Now tell the class about your holiday. Listen to the other students' holiday plans. Then decide which holiday sounds the most interesting.

Facts and figures

Look at the map. Which countries are on the map?
What information does it give you?

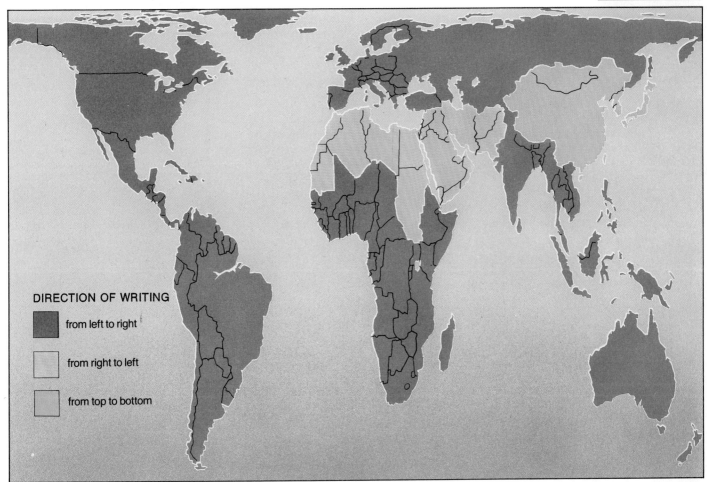

DIRECTION OF WRITING

- from left to right
- from right to left
- from top to bottom

Now look at these different scripts. Do you recognise them?

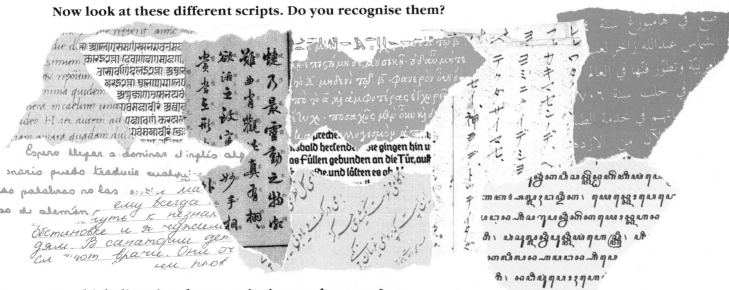

In which direction do you write in your language?
Does everybody in your country use the same language and script?

1

Look at this diagram to help you to understand the sentences.

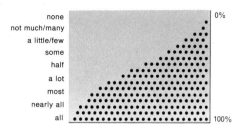

1 In all of the countries in South America, people write...
2 In most of the countries in the map, people write ...
3 But in some of them, people write ...
4 In a few of them, the script goes ...
5 But none of the countries have a script which goes ... !

Now look at the map on page 29 again and use the information to complete the sentences. Compare your answers with a partner's.

2

Look at this map showing the richer and poorer nations of the world.

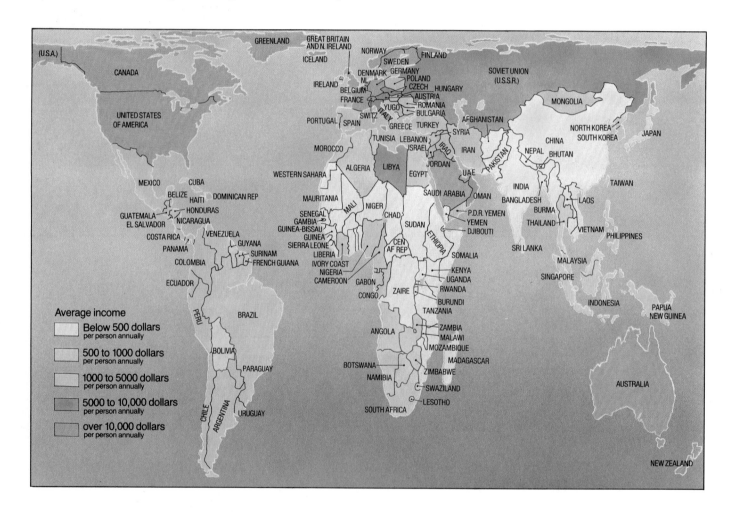

Complete these sentences about the map, using ... *all of, most of, a lot of, some of, a few of, not much/many of or none of.*

1 ...... the African nations are very poor.
2 ...... the nations in South America have an annual income of over $1000 per person.
3 ...... the richer nations are in the north.
4 ...... the nations in Europe have an annual income of over $10,000 per person.
5 ...... the poorer nations are south of the Equator.
6 ...... the nations in South America have an annual income of between $500 and $1000 per person.
7 ...... the African nations have an annual income of over $10,000 per person.

3

**Look at these 'facts'. They are all wrong.
Try to correct them.**

1 None of the world's capital cities
are on the coast.
2 A lot of the traffic in the UK travels
on the left-hand side of the road.
3 Most of the world's languages have more
words than English.
4 None of the world's coffee comes from
South America.
5 Most of the countries in Europe have
English as a first language.
6 All of the countries in Asia have four seasons.

 **Compare your answers with a partner,
then listen and check your answers.**

**Now write some wrong 'facts' about your country.
Write about traffic, cities, accommodation, languages.**

Ask your partner to correct your 'facts'.

4

**Here are some results of a department store's customer survey.
Look at it quickly and think about these questions.**

- What is the subject of the survey?
- How many customers answered the
  questions?
- Why do you think the department
  store did the survey?

 Work in pairs.

Ⓐ Turn to page 115.

**Ⓑ Look at the customer survey
again. Ask your partner questions
to find out the missing
information.**

Example
What do seventy of the customers wear
for work?

How many of the customers prefer
natural fibres?

**Now answer your partner's
questions.**

CUSTOMER SURVEY Questions		Answers	Customers
1	What kind of clothes do you usually wear for work?	Casual clothes.	19
			70
		Special clothes (e.g. uniform)	11
			50
2	What kinds of fibres do you prefer?	Natural fibres	
		Mixed fibres	
3	What colours do you prefer?	Light colours	11
			22
		A mixture of light and dark colours	
4	Do you feel unhappy about wearing leather or fur?	Yes	95
		No	
5	How do you wash your clothes?	In a washing-machine at home	83
		At a launderette	17
			0
			57
6	What feature do you look for in particular when you are choosing new clothes?	Style	15
		Quality	

5

Look at the results of the survey again. Decide if the numbers mean *all of* the customers, *most of* the customers etc., and complete this report on the survey.

One hundred regular customers in our store have completed a very revealing survey for us. ...... our customers wear smart clothes for work and only ...... them need special clothes.

Surprisingly, ... our customers prefer synthetic fibres and ...... them feel unhappy about wearing leather or fur.

For ...... them, a mixture of light and dark colours is the favourite, but ...... them prefer dark colours. ...... our customers think style is very important but ...... them look for comfort when they are choosing new clothes.

It seems that ...... our customers have a washing-machine at home and ...... them wash their clothes by hand.

over to you

Now ask the students in your class the survey questions.
Compare your results with a partner's. Write a report on the results of the survey.

6

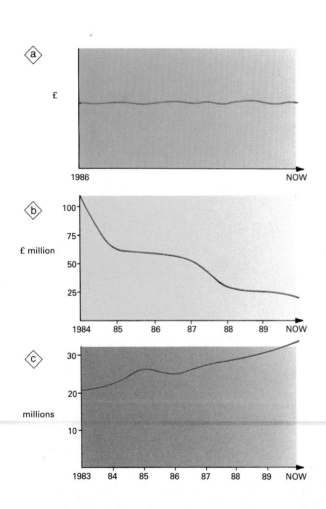

Listen to three short interviews about present trends in Britain.

Choose the right ending (a, b or c) for each sentence.

1 People
   a are buying less fur.
   b are buying more fur.
   c are not buying any fur.

2 The price of personal computers
   a is going up.
   b is staying about the same.
   c is going down.

3 For family holidays, more people
   a are staying at home.
   b are going abroad.
   c are going to another part of the UK.

Now decide which graph goes with each of your answers.

What can you say about present trends in your country?

7

Look quickly at this text about world trends.

● What kind of text is it?
● Where do you find texts like this?

◆ People are living longer...
◆ Salaries are increasing...
◆ Fewer people are eating meat nowadays...
◆ More people are wearing glasses...
◆ People are spending more time on leisure activities.

We come across statements like these every day in the media. But are these world trends completely unrelated, or are they linked in some way? For example, are people living longer because they are eating less meat? Sociologist, Caroline Roberts, has the answer to these and many other questions in her fascinating new book **Trends Connect**, available from good booksellers everywhere.

Read the text again and draw simple graphs for two or more of the trends.

Can you imagine how the trends are connected?

How do the trends compare with trends in your country?

Study points

a Listen and decide if the pairs of words you hear sound the same (s) or different (d).

wear   where
of   off
for   four
clothes   close
write   right

b Decide which word is correct in each sentence. Then listen and repeat.

1 I don't know where/wear he is.
2 Most of/off the people don't like fur.
3 Four/For of the countries are in the north.
4 They write/right from top to bottom.
5 They prefer casual close/clothes.

8

Look at this crowd scene. What can you say about the people?
What are they doing? What are they wearing? Use *most of, some of, a few of,* etc.

Grammar and Language

1 Quantifiers

Quantifiers are used to express the quantity or amount of something in relation to the whole.

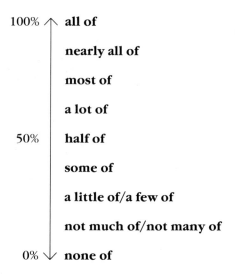

100% ↑	**all of**
	nearly all of
	most of
	a lot of
50%	**half of**
	some of
	a little of/a few of
	not much of/not many of
0% ↓	**none of**

You use a *little* of and *not much of* only with uncountable nouns. You use *a few of* and *not many of* only with plural countable nouns.
The other quantifiers can be used with both countable and uncountable nouns.

2 Present continuous for present trends

You can use the present continuous to indicate present trends and developments, particularly if the situation was different in the past and will possibly change in the future.

The price of computers	**is** not	**increasing.**
Computer prices	**are** not	

Where people live

Where would you like to live? Look at these homes.
Match the photos with the words below.

bungalow detached house semi-detached house flats terraced house

Which of these things has each home got? Make a list for each one.

roof gate front door chimney garden steps window garage curtains

1

Listen to Rita and Tom talking about four of the homes on page 35.

- Which homes are they talking about?
- What can you say about the other home?

Work in pairs.

Ⓐ **Choose one of the houses and study it carefully.**

Ⓑ **Ask questions to find out which house your partner has chosen.**

Example

Ⓑ Has it got a chimney/any chimneys?

Ⓐ Yes it has.

Ⓑ It's b!

2

Work in pairs.

Ⓐ **Turn to page 115.**

Ⓑ **Look at the advertisement for Global Village and make a note of its features under these headings.**

location	buildings	transport

Retire in Global Village style!

Retirement with all the advantages of country life just 50 miles (80km) from the capital. Impossible? No! Global Village puts this - and more - within your reach. Global village is set in beautiful surroundings in the heart of the Hampshire countryside, but, with regular bus and train services to London, the big city's never far away! Now available in Global Village are a number of superb detached retirement bungalows. Each one has a fully-fitted kitchen, living-room, bathroom with bath and shower, separate toilet and - so that there is plenty of room for guests - two spacious bedrooms. They are now for sale at last year's prices. So, hurry! Don't waste this unique opportunity! Call us on 200218.

Now answer your partner's questions about Global Village.

Example

Ⓐ Is there a bus service?

Ⓑ Yes, there is.

Ask your partner questions to find out what the area was like before. Use this table to help you. Make notes.

Was Were	there	a any	...?

Now turn to page 115. Was the area as you imagined?

3

Look at these plans of three bungalows. Try to name the rooms.

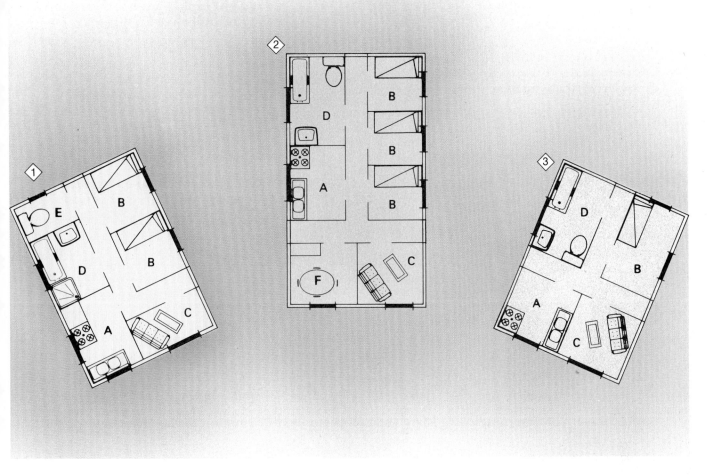

Read the advertisement for Global Village carefully and decide which of the bungalows is typical of the village.

4

Find the words or expressions in the advertisement which correspond to these definitions.

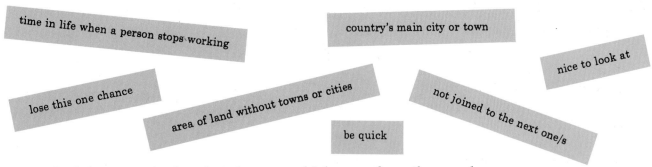

time in life when a person stops working

country's main city or town

nice to look at

lose this one chance

area of land without towns or cities

not joined to the next one/s

be quick

Now find the nouns in the advertisement which come from these verbs.

retire   live   reach   surround   sell

5

Complete this definition with the right word from the advertisement in exercise 2.

a ▮▮▮▮ is someone who is staying in your home or is at your party or wedding because you invited them.

Listen to Helena inviting four people to her party and put these expressions in the order that you hear them.

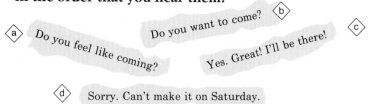

a Do you feel like coming?

b Do you want to come?

c Yes. Great! I'll be there!

d Sorry. Can't make it on Saturday.

e Would you like to come?

f Sorry, Helena. I'd love to come but I'm afraid I'm going to be busy that evening.

- How many people can't come to the party?
- Which is the most formal invitation?
- In what way is reply f more polite than reply c?

Study points

a Put eight capital letters, two commas and four full stops in this text.

there was a robbery at the new italian restaurant in green acre at 3 o'clock on wednesday afternoon the three robbers escaped with £2,000 the owner says that one of the men had long hair and a beard the man was carrying a large plastic bag and an umbrella

b Now decide where to put capital letters and full stops in this text.

these stylish modern flats in central london all have a fully-fitted kitchen spacious living-room three bedrooms and a bathroom with toilet there is plenty of parkland but the flats are well situated for local shops and services by next year, there will be a new underground station just three minutes' walk away

6

Look at this invitation to Helena's party and complete the information in the chart below.

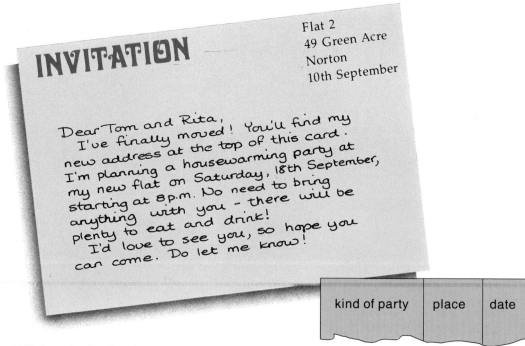

INVITATION

Flat 2
49 Green Acre
Norton
10th September

Dear Tom and Rita,
I've finally moved! You'll find my new address at the top of this card. I'm planning a housewarming party at my new flat on Saturday, 18th September, starting at 8 p.m. No need to bring anything with you – there will be plenty to eat and drink!
I'd love to see you, so hope you can come. Do let me know!

kind of party	place	date	time

- Will there be food at the party?
- How does Helena show that she wants a reply?

Imagine that it is your birthday soon. Write to a friend and invite him/her to your party.

7

Listen to this telephone conversation.

- Who is speaking?
- What has happened?

Listen again and complete Tom's sentences.

Helena	You probably went wrong at the Saver Supermarket.
Tom	Helena ..... that we ..... wrong at the Saver Supermarket.
Helena	You have to take the second turning on the left.
Tom	She ..... we ..... take the second turning on the left.
Helena	You'll see the bank on the left.
Tom	She ..... we ..... a bank on the left.
Helena	And my flat is opposite the bank.
Tom	And her flat ..... opposite the bank.

Mark the differences between Tom's and Helena's sentences.

Now find where Tom and Rita are on the map and follow the instructions to find Helena's flat.

Tom and Rita are travelling in this direction

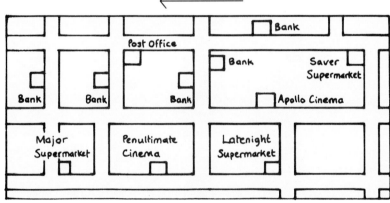

8

Work in groups of three.

Ⓐ Use the invitation you wrote for exercise 6. Give it to **Ⓑ**

Ⓑ Refuse the invitation and whisper an excuse to **Ⓒ**.

Example
I'm sorry I can't come. I have to work on Saturdays.
I'm sorry I can't come. I'll be on holiday then.

Ⓒ Tell **Ⓐ** why **Ⓑ** can't come.

Example
He/She says he/she has to work on Saturdays.
He/She says he'll/she'll be on holiday then.

Grammar and Language

1   There + *be*

If you want to talk about the existence or presence of something, you can precede it with *there* as the subject + 3rd person singular or plural *of be*.

Is/Was		a shop?			**is/was** a shop.
Are/Were	there	any shops?	**There**		**are/were** some shops.
Will		**be**	a shop? any shops?		**will be** a shop. some shops.

2   Reported speech: reporting verb in present

When you report something that someone is saying/often says/believes, you use the present tense of a reporting verb *say, think, know, believe*. You usually have to change the pronoun/ possessive adjective.

You can use *that* after the reporting verb.

You went wrong at the supermarket.
My flat is opposite the bank.

Helena **says** (that)	*we* went wrong at the supermarket. *her* flat is opposite the bank.

A way of life

Look at these people.
What are they doing? These words will help you.

| fish carve drive pick play bake |

What can you say about the people's lifestyles?

- Are their lives easy or hard?
- When do they get up/go to bed?
- How much time do they spend indoors/outside?

1

Listen to a TV interview on tape and decide which of the people on page 41 is speaking.

All these statements are false.
Listen to the interview again and correct them.

1 Pat was unhappy in her teaching career.
2 She lives and works in the city.
3 She lives alone.
4 She buys most of her food at the supermarket.
5 Her favourite activity is gardening.
6 Pat is reading a book on the self-sufficient way of life.

Would you like Pat's way of life?

2

Describe what Pat does in a typical day.
Use the words below to help you.

make   collect   grind

bread   eggs   butter   wheat

Now look at these scenes from a typical day.
What is Pat doing in each scene?

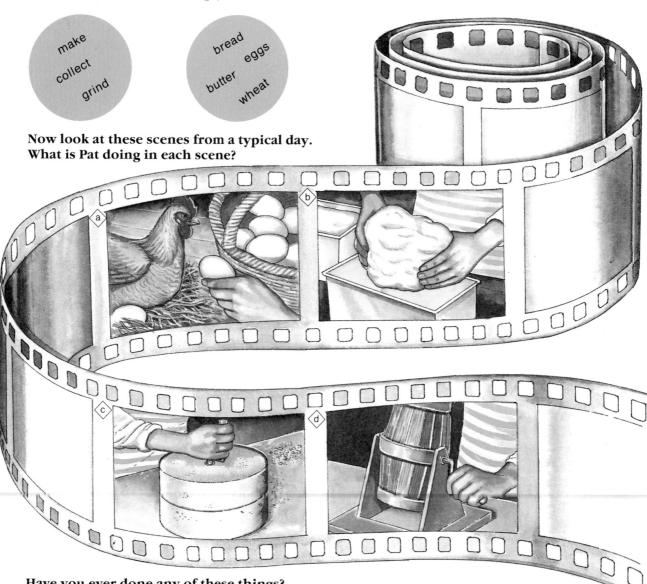

Have you ever done any of these things?
What other things do you think Pat does in a typical day?

3

Look at Pat's recipe for country vegetable bake and put the pictures in order.

Ingredients

2 onions, peeled and chopped
6 tomatoes, peeled and sliced
3 carrots, peeled and sliced
2 large potatoes, peeled and thinly sliced
1 cup fresh herbs, chopped
1 cup hot vegetable stock
3 slices brown bread made into breadcrumbs
150g grated cheese
25g butter for frying
salt and pepper

Method

1 Fry onions in butter in a metal casserole.
2 Remove from heat. Add vegetables and herbs in layers.
3 Season vegetable stock with salt and pepper and pour over vegetables.
4 Mix breadcrumbs and cheese and sprinkle on top.
5 Bake in a medium oven for about 45 minutes until the topping is golden brown.

What ingredients can you see here?

Are they right for the recipe?
Use *too much/ too many, enough, not enough* in your answers.
Example
There aren't enough tomatoes. You need six for the recipe.
The are too many potatoes. You only need two.
There's too much bread. You only need three slices.

4

Look at this magazine article quickly.

- How many people live in London?
- How many people in London work at night instead of during the day?

Work with a partner and list as many night jobs as you can think of. You have three minutes!
Make a class list of night jobs.

Night work!

London has a population of approximately 7,000,000. This number increases enormously during the day when millions of commuters go to work. London is much quieter and less busy at night. But work does not stop then! It is estimated that approximately 45,000 people have night jobs in the city. So, what kinds of jobs do people do at night?

Read another part of the magazine article about one of London's night workers and complete the information chart.

Jean Wilson

I work as a producer for Breakfast Time Television. I start work at 4 a.m. every day! Of course, this means that my lifestyle is a bit different from most people's.

I usually go to bed between about 6 and 7 in the evening. (I like to make sure that I get enough sleep because I have to get up at 2.30 in the morning and be at the studios at 3.45!) So, when I'm getting into bed,

most people are thinking about going out for the evening after a hard day's work.

I never have enough time to go out in the evening. But I finish work at 10 in the morning, so I have a nice long afternoon and I usually meet a few friends or go to the the cinema, or simply relax at home. I sometimes get tired of working at night, but I love my job and the people are so friendly.

Name:	
Job:	
Gets up at:	
Arrives at the studios at:	
Starts work at:	
Finishes work at:	
Goes to bed at:	

Work with a partner and ask questions to check that you have the same information.

Example
What does Jean do?

Answer these questions about Jean's lifestyle and then answer the same questions about your lifestyle.

1 Does she get enough sleep?
2 Does she have enough time to go out or meet friends in the evening?
3 Does she have enough time to relax in the afternnon?

Look at the article again. List the good things and the bad things about Jean's way of life. How does Jean's life differ from Pat's? Which lifestyle would you prefer?

Read sentences 1 - 5 and spot the difference in each sentence.

1 I always go to the cinema on Saturday.
2 I usually go to the cinema on Saturday.
3 I often go to the cinema on Saturday.
4 I sometimes go to the cinema on Saturday.
5 I never go to the cinema on Saturday.

Now match sentences 1 - 5 with sentences a - e.

a I go about four or five times a year on Saturday.
b I go every Saturday.
c I go to the theatre every Saturday, not the cinema.
d I go nearly every Saturday.
e I go every other Saturday

How do you spend your free time?
Write five sentences with *always, usually, sometimes, often, never*.
Compare your sentences with a partner's.
Do you spend your free time in the same way?

Study points	

a Listen to these words and notice the sounds of the letters in bold type.

always   usually   often   sometimes   never

b Now group these words under the words above.

friendly   off   enough   ten   up   hunt
during   come   university   health   call
exercise   many   spend   love   lucky
producer   check   student   four   let

Listen and check.

7

Listen to Linda Walters, a teacher, and Robert Michaels, an engineer, talking about their lifestyles.
Decide which diagram represents which person's lifestyle.

KEY

☐ Free time/time spent at home

☐ Time spent at work

☐ Time spent travelling

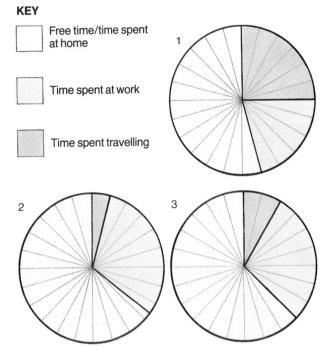

1

2   3

Listen again to check.

Now look at the other diagram.
Work with a partner and write about the person's lifestyle.
What kind of job do you think the person has?

over to you

Now write some sentences about your lifestyle and draw a diagram.
Give the diagram to your partner. Your partner must write about your lifestyle.
When he/she has finished, check his/her sentences.

8

Work in a group. Put the pictures into three 'healthy lifestyle' categories: exercise, food and drink, relaxation.

Now add as many other things as possible to each category.
You have five minutes!

You now have a 'healthy lifestyle' checklist.
Ask a partner questions to find out about his/her lifestyle.

Do you eat/drink enough...?
Do you eat/drink too much/many...?
How often do you...?
How many hours a day/week do you...?
How much... do you... a day/week?

Does your partner get enough exercise/the right kind of food and drink/enough relaxation?

Grammar and Language

1 Simple present v. present continuous

You can use the simple present to talk about regular actions, routines and general truths. You sometimes add an adverb of frequency to reinforce or clarify your statement.
You can use the present continuous to talk about actions in progress now and present trends and developments.

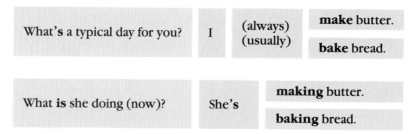

| What's a typical day for you? | I | (always) (usually) | **make** butter. |
| | | | **bake** bread. |

| What **is** she doing (now)? | She's | **making** butter. |
| | | **baking** bread. |

2 *enough* before nouns

You can use *enough* before plural countable nouns and uncountable nouns to say whether there is a sufficient number/amount.

| There | is/isn't | **enough** | salt | for the recipe. |
| | are/aren't | | tomatoes | |

3 Determiners: *too much / too many*

You can use *too much* with uncountable nouns and *too many* with plural countable nouns to show that there is/are more than enough.

| There | is **too much** bread | for the recipe. |
| | are **too many** potatoes | |

A funny thing happened ...

Paul had a terrible day yesterday. What happened?
Put the pictures in the right order.

Use the pictures and some of these words to describe Paul's day.

| break down | crash | fall across | go home | go to work | knock over | late |

1

Listen to Paul talking about his day and check the order of the pictures.

Listen again and complete the sentences below, putting the verb in brackets in the correct tense.

Example

I *was driving* (drive) to work when the car *broke down* (break down).

1 I ...... just ...... (walk) through the door when my boss ...... (come) out of her office.
2 I ...... (sit) on the edge of my desk when I ...... (reach) for my cup of coffee and ...... (knock) it over.
3 I ...... (drive) home through the storm when suddenly a tree ...... (fall) across the road. I ...... (crash) right into it.

Listen again and check your answers.

2

Divide the verbs from exercise 1 into two groups.

Actions in progress in the past	Sudden events in the past
I was driving	the car broke down

over to you

Which of these accidents has happened to you? Discuss with a partner.

● you were in a car crash
● you cut your finger
● you fell off a ladder
● you burnt yourself
● you were in a lift that stopped between floors

What were you doing when the accident happened? Write sentences.

Example

I was painting the bathroom ceiling when I fell off the ladder.

3

Look at the picture of a car accident. You were standing at point X when the accident happened. The police are interviewing you. Put these words in the right order to make their first question.

of - the - doing - time - at - were - what - you - the - accident?

Ⓐ **Try to memorise the information in the picture. You have two minutes.**

Ⓑ **Imagine you are a police officer. Think of questions to test your partner's memory.**

Example

Who was waiting at the bus stop?

4

Look at these statements about the picture. Decide which are true and which are false. Correct the false statements.

Example
The old lady was crossing the road.
The old lady wasn't crossing the road. She was waiting at the bus stop.

1 The young boy was opening the car door.
2 A tall man was getting off a bus.
3 A dog was running across the road.
4 Some children were riding bicycles.
5 Three women were waiting at the traffic lights.

5

**Look at these adjectives.
Put them into groups under
the headings below.**

shady	shadowy		well-lit
boiling	cool	shining	baking
freezing	bright	gloomy	warm

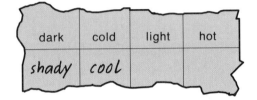

dark	cold	light	hot
shady	cool		

**Now add any other adjectives you know.
Compare your word groups with a partner's.**

Work with a partner. Ⓐ Think of a place. Give one adjective associated with it. Ⓑ Try to guess the place. Ⓐ Give a second adjective. Ⓑ Guess again.

Example   Ⓐ noisy
               Ⓑ Is it a market?
               Ⓐ No, it isn't. - crowded
               Ⓑ Is it an airport?
               Ⓐ No. - athletic
               Ⓑ Is it a football stadium?
               Ⓐ Yes, it is.

6

Listen to this true story and put the pictures in the correct order.

**Picture 6 is missing. How do you think the story ended?
Listen again and note down adjectives which mean:**

dark - not nice - frightening

Now try and answer these questions about the story.

- Where were Judith and her friends?
- What was the atmosphere like?
- Where did the door marked *Toiletten* lead?
- How did Judith feel when she ran back into the café?
- What did one of Judith's friends do?

**Read the text and check your answers.
How did the story end?**

A funny thing happened ...

... to Judith Doyle when she was on holiday in Germany last year. One ▓▓▓▓, Judith was sitting chatting to friends in a bar. It was a strange ▓▓▓, damp, gloomy and a little unfriendly. But this did not really worry ▓▓ until she was on her way to the toilet. The door marked *Toiletten* led into a ▓▓▓, dark corridor. She was feeling a little nervous, <u>so</u> she hurried along the ▓▓▓▓▓. She got the shock of her life when she suddenly came across a ▓▓▓, ghostly hand sticking out

through a window into the corridor. Terrified, Judith turned ▓▓ raced back to her friends in the bar, <u>but</u> their table was empty. She ▓▓ panic-stricken by now. Then she spotted them by the food counter. Still shaking, ▓▓ rushed up to them <u>and</u> told them about the hand. One of ▓▓ friends decided to go and see for herself. She soon came back, and the others ▓▓ that she was laughing. The 'hand' was really a rubber glove hanging on a broom handle!

Read the text again and fill in the gaps. Can you think of a title for the story?

8

Look at these words which are underlined in the text in exercise 7.

> and   but   so

These are examples of words used to join sentences together.

Join these sentences together, using *and*, *but* or *so*.

1 I wanted to go past the window.
   I was too frightened.

2 I wanted to leave.
   I couldn't find the door.

3 Maria explained everything to me.
   I laughed.

4 The corridor was very dark.
   I turned on the light.

9

Look at these notes.
They tell another story.

- a funny thing happened
- a party last week
- hot, crowded
- went into the garden
- bright light
- very quiet
- suddenly a man's voice ...

Use the notes to write out the story in full.
**Can you think of an ending? The story in exercise 7
will help you. Use the past continuous and past
simple and the linking words _and, but_ and _so_.**

Use as many adjectives as possible.

**Read your story to a partner and
compare endings.**

a Which spelling is correct?

1 happenning - happening
2 stopping - stoping
3 trying - triing
4 driving - driveing
5 comeing - coming

b Look at these sentences.

I read the sign. Then I opened the door.

**Now look at ways of linking these
sentences using _before_ and _after_.**

I read the sign before I opened the door.
After I read the sign, I opened the door.

**Make each sentence into two.
Begin the second one with _Then_.**

1 The train left before I arrived.
2 I saw the car before it stopped.
3 After I got home, he phoned me.
4 After we had lunch, we left.

10

**Work in groups. Your teacher will give each student in your
group a piece of paper like this.**

CUE: ... AND GOT ON.	I was cycling down a really steep hill when I saw a car. It was coming fast around the corner.

**Look at your own piece of paper. It has two things on it - a cue and a sentence.
Find out the meaning of any new words. Listen carefully for your cue.**

When you hear it, read your sentence.

Grammar and Language

1   Past continuous / simple past

You can use the past continuous with the simple past to contrast a situation or an action in progress with a sudden event. You usually use *when* to connect the situation with the event.

I **was driving**	to work home	**when**	the car **broke down.** a tree **fell** across the road.

2   Linking words: *and, but, so*

You can use *and, but, so* to join clauses and to show the relationship between them.

a   You can use *and* to link two clauses when you want to show that the first action mentioned happens/happened before the other.
You do not usually repeat the subject in the second clause.

She rushed up to them	**and**	told them about it.

b   You can use *but* to link two clauses when you want to contrast the second fact with the first in some way.

She raced back to her friends,	**but**	their table was empty.

c   You can use *so* to link two clauses when you want to show that the second action is a result of the first.

She was feeling nervous	**so**	she hurried away ...

Help at hand

Look at this month's edition of _City Lights_. What is the special feature?

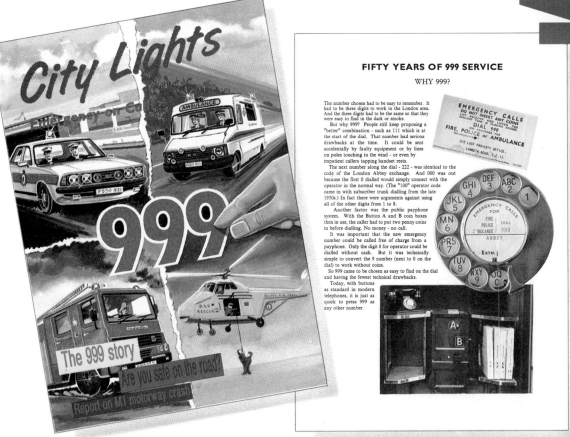

What are the four emergency services?
What number must you dial for these services?
What is the number in your country?

1

Listen to these emergency '999' telephone calls.
Answer these questions for each call.

- Which services do the callers require?
- What is the emergency?
- Where is the emergency?

2

Listen to reporter, Susie Harper, interviewing an ambulance driver for _City Lights_.

Put her questions in the right order.

a What did you do yesterday?
b How often do you have to work at night?
c How many of these accidents are road accidents?
d Was yesterday a typical day?
e How many accidents do you deal with every day?

Listen again and make a note of the driver's answers.

Now use questions like Susie's to interview a partner. Your partner works for one of the emergency services.

3

The editor is correcting some sentences from Susie's article.

Choose the correct word or words for each sentence.

1 When there's an accident, people usually (are phoning/phone) for an ambulance.

2 The driver of the car (wasn't wearing/ didn't wear) his seat belt when the accident (was happening/happened).

3 We (drove/were driving) along the main road when we (were seeing/saw) the accident.

4 Ambulance drivers always (wear/are wearing) a uniform.

5 The number of accidents is increasing (and/but) there (isn't/aren't) enough doctors to deal with all the emergencies.

4

Now the editor wants to rewrite some of the sentences in the story.

Complete the new sentences.

Example
There are six patients and only five beds.
There aren't enough beds.

1 Each ambulance has got at least two oxygen tanks.
There are...

2 "He fell downstairs," she says.
She says that...

3 More accidents will happen in the future.
There will be...

4 There are only three hospitals with enough beds.
Only a few hospitals ...

5 The car hit her when she was crossing.
She was...

5

Look at the video still from *City Lights* of a robbery about to take place in a newsagent's. Then answer these questions.

- Who are the people?
- What is happening?
- What do you think is going to happen?

Susie talked to a witness about what happened.

Choose the correct words from the list below to complete the witness's story.

I was ...(1)... some magazines in the newsagent's when suddenly the door ...(2)... with a bang. A man wearing a black mask and carrying a ...(3)... came in. He ran up to the counter and ...(4)..., "Hands up! Give me the money or I'll shoot." The shop assistant was very frightened and gave him some money. I...(5)... move. The masked man stuffed the money ...(6)... his jacket pocket, ...(7)... ran out. Another man ...(8)... on a motor-bike. I ...(9)... to the telephone and dialled 999 for the police, but it ...(10).. too late. The robbers had already escaped.

1 buy - buying - bought - taking
2 opening - opened - open - closed
3 book - bag - gun - pen
4 shouting - was shouting - shouted - shout
5 don't - didn't - doesn't - wasn't
6 into - on - out - from
7 when - so - and - but
8 waited - was waiting - has waited - waiting
9 was going - went - going - go
10 is - were - are - was

6

Look at the article from *City Lights* about a plane crash near a motorway.

Match the sentence halves and complete the article. (The sentence halves on the right are in the correct order.) Use the diagram to help you.

It was a cold winter's day when the plane left London. The passengers were beginning to relax after a smooth take-off and were looking forward to a short, comfortable flight...

1 Before it could land	a when passengers noticed that the left engine was on fire.
2 Fire, police and ambulance services	b to make an emergency landing at a nearby airport.
3 The pilot turned the plane	c the right engine failed.
4 The plane was flying northwards	d the plane crashed in a muddy field near the motorway.
5 As the plane was approaching the airport,	e rushed to the scene of the accident.

The emergency services did a marvellous job

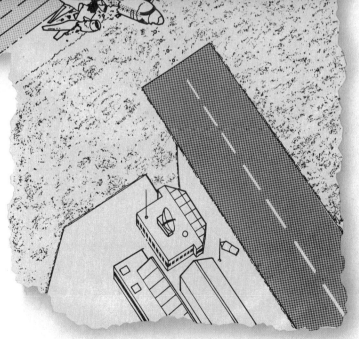

Study points

Group these expressions under the headings 'simple present' and 'simple past'.

she held	we take	we wear
he falls	you said	you tell
they drive	they found	I put
they came	she hears	he sat
she left	it flew	I write

If you want to check in a dictionary, which word do you have to look up in each case?

How do you think the story ended?

7

Susie heard an emergency telephone call to the local ambulance service.
Listen and put the pictures in the right order.

The telephonist is giving details to the ambulance driver over the radio.
Listen and fill in the missing words.

"Hello, Jim. I've got a lady on the other phone who says a car ...... down on a ...... crossing. The car ...... round the ...... when the old lady ...... without looking. The ...... the old lady and then a motor-bike ...... the back of .... She says it ...... just ...... the ABC cinema in the centre of town."

8

Susie arranged to interview Jim at the ambulance station. These were Jim's directions. Follow them on the map.

Come out of the station into North Street, turn right and then left into Middle Lane. Take the first turning on the right and walk to the crossroads. Turn left and the ambulance station is halfway down on the right.

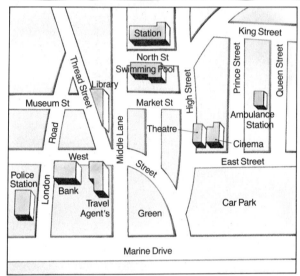

- Where did Susie get to?
- Did she walk further than necessary?

Now write the correct directions.

9

Work in groups. In each group, two students are suspected of the robbery in exercise 5. The others are the police.

SUSPECTS - Work together and decide:

- where you were at the time of the crime.
- what you were wearing.
- what you were doing.
- who you met.
- any other details.

POLICE - Prepare your questions and interview the supects separately. Ask:

- what they were wearing.
- what they were doing.
- where they were at the time of the crime.
- who they were with.

Take notes while each suspect answers. Then compare their answers. Are they telling the truth?

What's your line?

Look at the people in the pictures and study the questionnaire.

farmer

teacher

bank manager

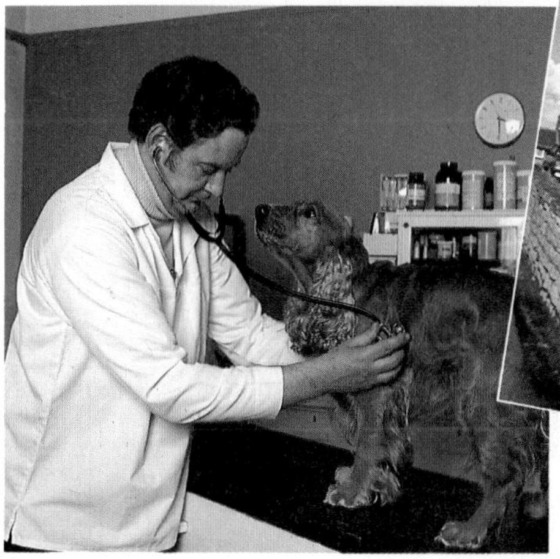

vet

police officer

pilot

JOBQUEST 2000

Complete sections A and B of the questionnaire. Let our computer help you find the perfect career.

A: SKILLS AND QUALITIES

I'm good at ☑
I'm not very good at ☒

1 working with machines. ☑
2 working with my hands. ☑
3 organising my work. ☒
4 driving. ☑
5 typing. ☒
6 taking decisions. ☒
7 managing people. ☒
8 being punctual. ☒

B: LIKES AND DISLIKES

I like ☑
I don't like ☒

1 working alone. ☑
2 working in an office. ☒
3 working outside. ☑
4 working with children. ☒
5 working with animals. ☑
6 helping people. ☒
7 working at weekends. ☑
8 getting up in the morning. ☑

Which person do you think completed the questionnaire?

1

Listen to a Jobquest interview with Sue James a few years ago and answer
six questions in the questionnaire for her.
Check your answers with a partner.
Now decide which of the photos on page 57 shows Sue James in her present job.

Listen to Sue James again. Write down two things she likes doing in her spare time.

2

Answer the questionnaire for one of the other people in the pictures.
Tell a partner about the person. Your partner must guess who the person is.

Example
This person likes working outside. He/She isn't very good at ..., but ...

Now listen to your partner. Who is he/she describing?

over to you

Use the questionnaire to ask your partner some questions.

Example
Ⓐ Do you like working at weekends?
Ⓑ Yes, I do./No, I don't.
Ⓐ Are you good at organising your work?
Ⓑ Yes, I am./No, I'm not.

Write about your partner.

Example
He/She likes helping people ... He/She isn't very good at working with machines, but ...

Tell the class about your partner and decide on the 'perfect career' for him/her.

3

Look at the picture and the advertisement and think about these questions.

- What is the advertisement for?
- Who is the person in the picture?
- Who is she talking to?
- What is she talking about?

LEAVING SCHOOL?
WANT A CAREER IN BANKING? ...

InterBank International is
looking for a young person
to join their professional
staff as a trainee. If you are
16 - 19 years old and
want to work for a large
banking organisation,
phone the Manager
for further details.
InterBank International
Tel: 2530 101

4

Listen to the bank manager's conversations with (1) Kenneth Brown and (2) Diane Perry and study the chart.
Some of the information is incorrect. Correct it as you listen.

	good at ...			likes ...		enjoys ...	
Y = yes N = no	spelling	typing	working in an office	writing letters	talking to people	swimming	playing tennis
1 Kenneth Brown	N	Y	Y		Y	Y	N
2 Diane Perry	N	N	N	Y	Y		
3 .... Parker	Y				Y	N	

Write correct sentences about Kenneth Brown or Diane Perry.

Example
Kenneth Brown is good at spelling. He doesn't like ...

5

Person number 3 in the chart got the job at InterBank International.
Work with your partner to find the missing information.

Ⓐ Turn to page 116.

Ⓑ Look at the chart for person number 3 and answer your partner's questions.
Ask your partner questions to find the missing information from your chart.

Example
What is the person's first name?
Is she good at typing?

Write about person number 3.
Check to see if you and your partner have written the same.

over to you

Now complete the chart for yourself. Compare yourself with the three people in the chart. Who is the most similar to you?

6

Look at these three texts quickly.

- What kind of texts are they?
- Where can you find texts like these?

Gro Petersen from Norway is personal assistant to a senior executive in an oil company in Rotterdam. Gro speaks four languages fluently - Norwegian, English, French and German - and is planning to learn Japanese. Gro has to speak foreign languages well because her job takes her all over the world. Says Gro: "I'm lucky - I learn languages easily, so a new language is usually no problem for me!"

Christine Parker is 18 and lives in London. She has just started a job with InterBank International as a trainee and hopes to travel as much as possible with her new job. When she's not at work, Christine enjoys cooking and music. "In my kind of job you have to work carefully - but fast! That's why I enjoy relaxing properly in my spare time!"

Maurizio Donatini is 19 and comes from Venice. He is studying languages and his ambition is to be an interpreter. In his spare time, Maurizio enjoys walking, playing football and, in winter, skiing. "You have to work hard if you want to be successful," he says,"but relaxation is important, too."

Gerhard Müller is in his twenties and comes from

Read the texts carefully and answer these questions.

1 Who wants to work with languages?
2 Whose ambition is it to travel?
3 Who is going to learn another language?
4 Who enjoys different sports as hobbies?

7

Find sentences or expressions in the texts with similar meanings to the following.

Example
You have to be a careful worker. = *You have to work carefully.*
1 You have to be a hard worker.
2 Gro is a fluent speaker of four languages.
3 You have to be a fast worker.
4 Gro has to be good at speaking foreign languages.
5 It's easy for me to learn languages.

What differences do you notice between these sentences and the sentences in the texts?

8

Look at the lists below. Which qualities are important for each job? Make sentences.

Example
A scientist has to work carefully and think fast.

jobs
writer
dentist
engineer
scientist

'has to'
- work hard
- speak foreign languages well
- work carefully
- learn quickly
- make friends easily
- think fast

Compare your sentences with a partner's. Did you have the same ideas?
Why are these qualities important for the jobs?

Study points

Look at these words from the unit.

professional foreign punctual perfect successful

Put each word into one of these definitions.

1   People who are ...... arrive at a place at exactly the right time.
2   A ...... person is someone who has done well in his/her job or career.
3   A ...... worker is someone who has learnt the special skills necessary for a job.
4   Something that is ...... belongs to or comes from another country.
5   The '...... career' for someone is one which is ideal in every way.

9

Work with a partner.

Ⓐ **Look at the personal profiles in exercise 6 again. Choose one person.**

Ⓑ **Ask questions to find out who your partner has chosen.**

Example
Does the person have to speak languages well?

Work in groups and ask similar questions to find out about other students' jobs.

10

Look at this information about Gerhard Müller and write a personal profile for him.
(Use the personal profiles on page 60 to help you.)

Name	Gerhard Müller
Age	28
From	Hamburg, Germany
Job	dentist
Ambition	to work in Africa
Enjoys	tennis, swimming (in spare time)

Grammar and Language

1 Verbs/expressions with the gerund

Certain verbs and expressions can be followed by a gerund (*ing-* word).

She	**likes/doesn't like** **enjoys/doesn't enjoy** **is/is not** (very) **good at**	cook**ing**. work**ing** with children. learn**ing** languages.

Sometimes you can say the same thing simply by using a noun.

She	**likes/doesn't like** **enjoys/doesn't enjoy** **is/is not** (very) **good at**	languages.

2 Adverbs of manner

You use adverbs of manner with verbs to describe **how** something is done.

(How does she speak English?)	She speaks English	**fluently.** **carefully** **well.**

	Adjective	**Adverb**
To make an adverb of manner from an adjective, you usually add *ly*.	fluent proper bad	fluent**ly** proper**ly** bad**ly**
If an adjective ends in *y*, you change the *y* to *i* and add *ly*.	easy angry happy	eas**ily** angr**ily** happ**ily**
Some adjectives do not change to make the adverb.	fast hard	fast hard
In one case, you use a different word.	good	well

Preparations for the future

A large company is going to build a hotel and conference centre.
Look at the site and describe what it is like now.

Now say how you think it will change. Use the words below.

> traffic people buildings roads noisy beautiful clean natural
> busy peaceful dangerous colourful polluted crowded

Example
There will probably be more traffic. The area will be more polluted.

Which changes do you think will be positive and which will be negative?

1

Look at the two men in the picture on page 63.

- Who do you think they are?
- What are they doing?

 Listen to this conversation between the two men. Decide which of these statements are true and which are false. Correct the false statements.

1 Both of the men think that the hotel and conference centre will improve the area.
2 Both of the men have met the new employee.
3 The new employee is a qualified psychologist.
4 She already works for the company.

Listen again and match the sentence halves.

1 If the new employee is good,
2 The Hanging Gardens project will be complete in three years' time
3 If the Hanging Gardens project is successful,

a the company will develop the resort for tourism.
b if the company directors approve the plan.
c she will work on all the major projects in the future.

Write the sentences down and number them 1 - 3.

2

Look at the sentences you have written down in exercise 1 and answer these questions.

1 Is it certain that the new employee will be good?
2 Is it certain that the directors will approve the plan for the Hanging Gardens Centre?
3 Is it certain that the project will be successful?

Look carefully at the parts of the sentences which gave you your answers. What word begins them and what verb tense do they all have?

3

 Work in pairs.
Ⓐ **Look at page 115.**

Ⓑ **Study this plan for the Hanging Gardens Hotel and Conference Centre. Ask your partner questions to find the missing information.**

Example
What will be next to the office?

Hanging Gardens Centre PLAN 1

Car Park

Conference rooms

Office   Computer centre

Hanging Gardens Hotel and Conference Centre
- *planning information* -

Location: inland, 30km from coast and nearest major town

Climate: mainly dry, not much rain

Average temperatures: summer 22⁰C winter 10⁰C

Purpose of Centre: to provide hotel accommodation and conference facilities for up to 500 people

Can you see any problems with the present plan? Discuss it with a partner.
Think about the following things:

- natural daylight.
- noise from car park.
- position of the conference rooms.

Find out what the other students in the class think.

4

Read Ann Newman's analysis of the plan for the Hanging Gardens Centre.

- Does she think the plan is good?
- Why do you think she has written this analysis?

Analysis of Hanging Gardens plan

1 If the Centre is rectangular, some important areas will not have natural daylight. A circular design is usually ideal for this kind of project because all the rooms receive a maximum amount of light.

2 If the car park is so near the hotel accommodation, the noise of the cars will disturb the guests. It must not be near places where guests want to relax or sleep.

3 If the restaurant area is so close to the conference rooms, guests will not really relax at mealtimes. The restaurant must be further away from the conference rooms.

What problems does Ann see with the plan?
In exercise 3, did you and your partner see the same problems?
Study carefully the sentences which tell you what the problems are.

- How many clauses does each sentence have?
- Underline the verbs in each clause.

What recommendations does Ann make in her analysis?

5

Work in a group and decide how to complete these four sentences.

1 If the guests do not have the chance to take some exercise, they ...
2 Guests will need a quiet room if ...
3 If people have to get to the centre quickly, they ...
4 People will need a shaded area if ...

 Now listen to the tape. Were your ideas the same as or similar to Ann's? Make a note of four problems mentioned. Can you make any recommendations to solve these problems?

Example
1 The Hanging Gardens Centre needs a sports area/swimming pool.

Read this text carefully and study the underlined words. Decide what they refer to.

Example <u>its</u> = Cuandra

Cuandra is not an expensive resort, but <u>its</u> facilities are excellent. There is no shortage of hotels and restaurants and <u>they</u> put the customer first.

The resort development is proud of its recent achievements. <u>These</u> include an Olympic-type sports centre. Satisfied customers come back every year and <u>they</u> all tell us that it is <u>their</u> first choice.

If you want a relaxing or active holiday, Cuandra will offer you everything. *It is the ideal holiday resort.*

6

Study the new plan based on Ann's recommendations.

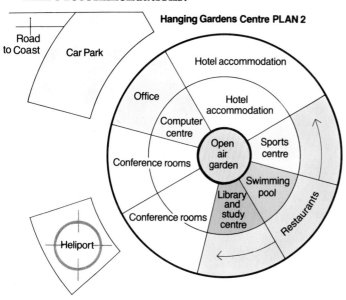

Hanging Gardens Centre PLAN 2

Road to Coast

Car Park

Hotel accommodation

Office

Hotel accommodation

Computer centre

Open air garden

Sports centre

Conference rooms

Swimming pool

Library and study centre

Conference rooms

Restaurants

Heliport

Is the plan better? Work with a partner and decide what problems you think this plan will cause. Write sentences.

Example
If the heliport is near the conference rooms, the noise will disturb the guests.

Work in groups and compare your ideas. Try to agree on the problems and then draw a new plan. How does your plan compare with the plans other groups have drawn?

7

Read the publicity notice about the Hanging Gardens Centre and decide which items in the pictures are necessary for visitors.

The Hanging Gardens Hotel and Conference Centre is situated inland, approximately 30km from the coast and the nearest major town. It is connected with the coast and the nearest large town by a superb new road and a frequent helicopter service. The climate is excellent. There is very little rain and the average temperature is 10^0C in winter and 22^0C in summer in this sunny area. The Hanging Gardens Centre has hotel and conference facilities for up to 500 guests. It has a well-equipped library and study centre and offers plenty of opportunity for relaxation with its modern sports centre and swimming pool. A first-class restaurant offers an international menu

Compare your answers with other students' answers.

Use your answers and the information in the text to write advice for visitors to the Hanging Gardens Centre. Think about:

climate	transport	relaxation	food	work

Example
If you want to read or study, you will find a well-equipped library.

8

Look at this information about a resort.

- In which part of the world is this resort?
- What kind of resort is it?

Work with a partner and write some advice for visitors to this resort.

over to you

Choose a resort in your country. Write some recommendations for visitors to the resort.

Example
If you go there in March, you will need an umbrella.

Give your sentences to your partner. Your partner must guess the details about the location and climate of the resort.

Location: on the coast, 5km from the capital city; good bus connections to the capital; near mountains

Climate: mainly dry; rainy months - January to March

Average temperatures:
Spring (March - May) 10°C
Summer (June - August) 20°C
Autumn (Sept - Nov) 12°C
Winter (Dec - Feb) 5°C

9

Look at the pictures showing seasons in different parts of the world. Match them with these words.

| spring summer autumn winter dry season rainy season |

① ③ ⑤ ④ ⑥ ②

What seasons do you have in your country?

Look at these words and put them into groups for the seasons in your country.

| hot cold rain(y) sun(ny) dry wet clear snow(y) frost(y) fog(gy) mild |

Use the words to talk or write about the seasons in your country.

Grammar and Language

First conditional

You can use the first conditional to talk about a future event/action/situation which is possible, but not certain.

	Conditional clause		Result clause		
If	Subject	Simple present	Subject	*will / will not*	Infinitive
If	Ann	succeeds,	she	**will/will not ('ll/won't)**	work on other projects.
	her plan		the company		

You can reverse the order of the conditional clause and the result clause without changing the meaning.

Result clause	Conditional clause
She**'ll** work on other projects	**if** her plan **is** successful.

What would you do ...?

Look at the picture.

- Where is the man?
- What has happened?
- What problems does he have?

What would you do if you were this man?
Use the pictures and the words below to help you.

boat shelter fire hunt fish sew build clothes

Example
I would catch fish for food.

Compare your list with a partner's. Agree on the three most important things.

1

Look at the photograph.

- What can you say about it?
- Where do you think it is?

🔊 **Listen to an interview with Anna Davis. Decide if the following statements are true or false, and correct the false ones.**

1 She was working as a secretary.
2 She phoned Australia.
3 The women are different ages.
4 The island was 800 kilometres from Fiji.
5 She went on an army course.

Listen again and answer the questions.

1 Where did she see the advertisement?
2 What did she remember about it?
3 How many other people also wanted to go to the island?
4 What did the women have in common?
5 What was the interviewer's last question?
   If I ...... to a remote island, what would I need?

2

Work with a partner. Use the words in the list to identify the objects in the pictures. Can you name them? Decide what you would use each object for.

hammer
knife
string
radio
paper
pen
clothes
binoculars
nails
shoes
books
saw
matches
mirror
spade
scissors

Make sure you know the meaning of the other words in the list.
Use a diconary to help you.

Choose ten of the objects to take to a remote island with you.
Compare your list with your partner's and agree on the five most important things.

3

Look at this extract from Anna's letter to Jenny in Australia.

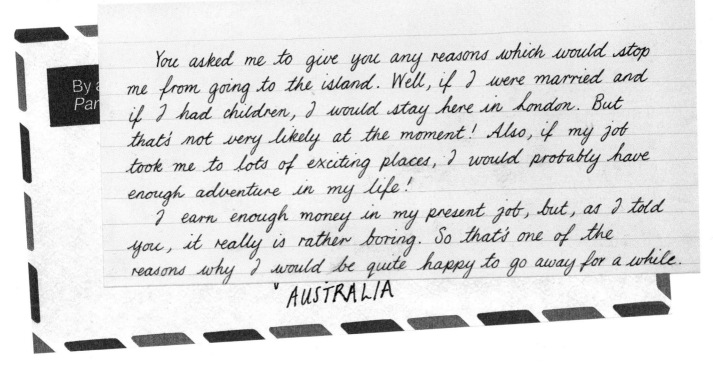

You asked me to give you any reasons which would stop me from going to the island. Well, if I were married and if I had children, I would stay here in London. But that's not very likely at the moment! Also, if my job took me to lots of exciting places, I would probably have enough adventure in my life!

I earn enough money in my present job, but, as I told you, it really is rather boring. So that's one of the reasons why I would be quite happy to go away for a while.

AUSTRALIA

Write full answers to these questions.

1 Is Anna married?
2 Does she have any children?
3 Does her job take her to exciting places?

Now write down the sentences from the letter which gave you the answers.
Compare your answers with the sentences from the letter.

Use the information in the letter to complete these sentences.

1 If Anna ......, she would not go to the island.
2 If Anna ......, she ...... not go to the island.
3 Also, if Anna's ......, she ...... not go to the island.

4

**Look at these questions. Match them with the best answers,
and then make full sentences with _if_.**

Example
1-d   If everybody spoke the same language, travelling would be easier.

What would happen if ...

1 everybody spoke the same language?
2 people only worked for one day a week?
3 the sun stopped shining?
4 nobody drove cars?
5 people were always unhappy?
6 people didn't have telephones?
7 people didn't take any exercise?

a The weather would never be warm.
b They would not be very healthy.
c The air would be cleaner.
d Travelling would be easier.
e The world would be a very sad place.
f They would write more letters.
g They would have a lot of spare time.

Check your sentences with a partner.
Then try to give your own answers to the questions.

5

Use the information you have about Anna Davis to complete this profile of her.

PERSONAL PROFILE   Yes   No
Name: Anna Davis
1   I live in a town/city.
2   I live in a hot country.
3   I work outside.
4   I work in an office.
5   I work in a factory.
6   I work in a school.
7   I am married.
8   I don't have any children.
9   I travel in my job.
10 I speak English.

Work with a partner.
Imagine what would happen if things were different. Write sentences about Anna.

Example
If she were married, she wouldn't go to the island.
If she didn't speak English, Jenny wouldn't be able to communicate with her.

over to you

Complete the personal profile for yourself and write about yourself in the same way.

Example
If I weren't married, I would spend less time at home.

Now compare yourself with a partner.

6

Look at sentences a - g in exercise 4 again and choose three of them.
Write new *if*-clauses for the sentences you have chosen.
Show them to a partner.
Your partner must match them with the correct answers from a - g.

Example
You have chosen: c ... The air would be cleaner.
Your new if-clause: If people didn't smoke, ...

Your partner reads your *if*-clause and matches it with answer c.

7

Read this newspaper article about Anna Davis carefully. Some of the information is wrong.
Find the wrong information. Check with a partner.
Rewrite the article with the correct information.

ISLAND HOME FOR ANNA

ANNA Kirby, a 25-year-old policewoman from Edinburgh, flew off to Australia today to join Jenny Andersen in Sydney.

The two women are about to begin a three-year adventure living on a Mediterranean island with their families.

Anna has been unemployed for a year, but is now looking forward to full-time employment on the island. Full-time employment? "Yes," Anna told reporters. "There will be plenty of work for both of us just finding food and making a home for ourselves!"

But why does Anna want to go such a long way from home? "Well, my present job is quite boring and I want some adventure in my life while I'm still young enough!"

How will she and Jenny communicate? "Oh, that will be a problem. I don't speak German, you see. It would be much easier if Jenny and I spoke the same language."

8

Look at these pictures and decide what the problem is in each one.

Look at these pieces of advice. Which advice would you give in each situation?

a If I were her, I would use some matches.
b If I were them, I would take a taxi.
c If I were them, I would go to the Sunnyside Hotel.
d If I were him, I would go to the doctor's.

Note down the expression which shows that somebody wants to give advice or make a suggestion.

What would you say for the other two pictures?

Now ask your partner to tell you about three problems that he/she has. Give advice in each case.

a Listen to the dialogue. Where does speaker B put the main stress?

A: If I were her, I'd take a radio with me.
B: Oh, I'd take a cassette player.

What does the second speaker mean?

a Good idea, but I'd take a cassette player, too.
or
b I don't agree with you. I'd take a cassette player instead of a radio.

Now listen again and repeat.

b Listen to six sentences and decide what you would do in each case. Use these words.

1 pencil   2 dried food
3 shampoo   4 books
5 motorbike   6 torch

Work with a partner. Your partner uses the words above to say what he/she would do.

Example
If I were her, I'd take a pencil with me.

Disagree with your partner and say what you would do.

Example
Oh, I'd take a pen.

9

What would you do if you won a million pounds? Make a list.

Example
If I won £1,000,000, I wouldn't go to work.

Exchange lists with your partner. Are your partner's ideas sensible or not? Advise him/her.

Example
If I were you, I'd continue to work.
If you stopped working, you'd be bored.

Grammar and Language

Second conditional

When you talk about an unlikely or impossible situation and you imagine its result, you can use the second conditional.

Conditional clause			Result clause		
If	Subject	Simple past	Subject	*would/would not*	Infinitive
If	I Tim they	**had** £1,000,000, **were** rich,	I he the family	**would/would not** (**'d/wouldn't**)	**stop** working.

NOTE: When *be* is the main verb in the conditional clause, the form is always *were*. You can reverse the order of the conditional clause and the result clause without changing the meaning.

Result clause	Conditional clause
Tim **would/would not** stop working	**if** he had £1,000,000.

Going green

Look at this poster about the environment and how we treat it.
Match the photos with the statements about the environment.

How GREEN is your world?

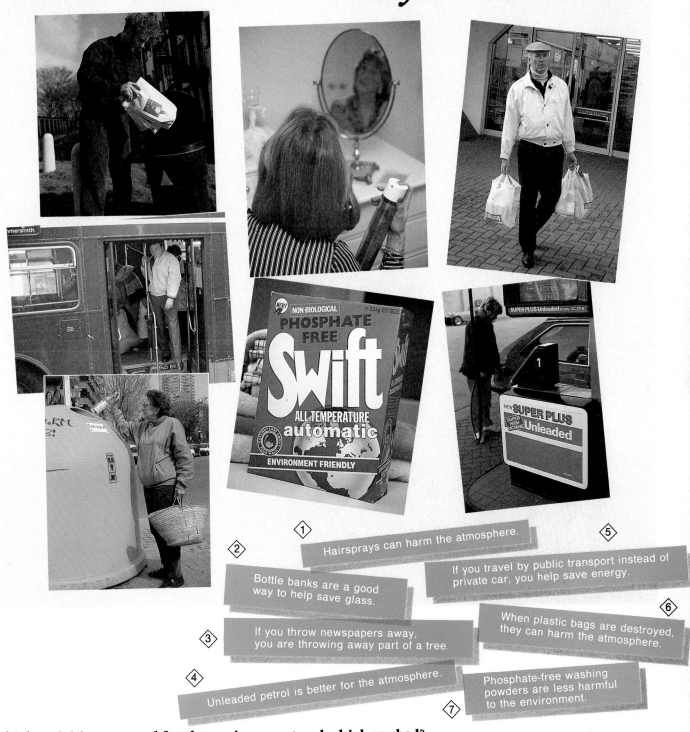

1 Hairsprays can harm the atmosphere.

2 Bottle banks are a good way to help save glass.

3 If you throw newspapers away, you are throwing away part of a tree.

4 Unleaded petrol is better for the atmosphere.

5 If you travel by public transport instead of private car, you help save energy.

6 When plastic bags are destroyed, they can harm the atmosphere.

7 Phosphate-free washing powders are less harmful to the environment.

Which activities are good for the environment and which are bad?
What does the title mean? Can you think of an alternative title?

1

Look at the poster again.
Choose a piece of advice for each photo.

1 Travel by public transport.
2 Don't throw newspapers away.
3 Use unleaded petrol.
4 Don't use an aerosol spray.
5 Re-use plastic carrier bags.
6 Use a phosphate-free washing powder.
7 Take your empty bottles to a bottle bank.

Now give the same advice in another way.

Example
Travel by public transport. *Don't travel by car.*
Don't use an aerosol spray. *Use an atomiser.*

 *over to you*

Which of the pieces of advice do you follow?
How green is your world?

How do you help to protect the environment?
Write sentences.

2

Look at this definition of *recycle*.

> If you recycle things that have already
> been used, you process them so that
> they can be used again.

Which two things mentioned in exercise 1
can you recycle?

 Listen to part of an interview with an
environmental officer. Were you right?
What else can you recycle?

Listen to the second part of the interview
about how we can save energy in the home.
Look at the pictures. What does the
environmental officer say about them?
Are they good or bad for the environment?

Listen to the interview again and fill in the
missing words in these sentences. Use *too*,
***enough* or *not ... enough*.**

1 We use ... much energy in the home.
2 Don't use ... much water in the bath.
3 Ten minutes in the shower should be ... time
   for anyone!
4 If you're ... warm ..., don't turn up the heating -
   put on an extra jumper.
5 If you're ... warm, take it off.
6 And don't forget that in summer, it's light ...
   to read until nine or ten in the evening
   without an electric light.

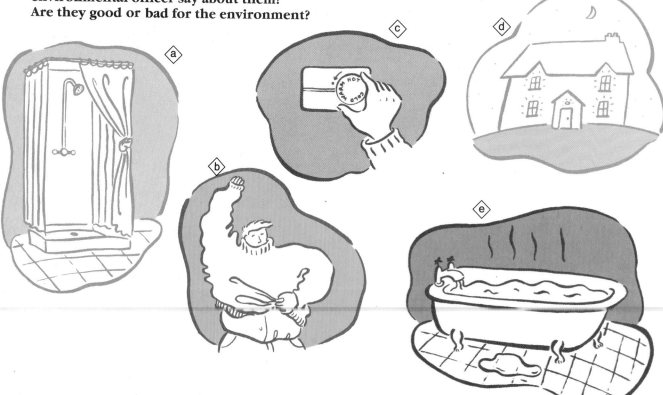

3

Look at these pieces of advice from the environmental officer.
Put the words in the right order.

1 newspapers/to a recycling/Give/company/.
2 small/as/envelopes/notepaper/Use/.
3 energy/save/Learn/to/.
4 instead of/Take/a bath/a shower/.
5 the/central/Turn/heating/down/.

Here are the interviewer's notes about what the environmental officer said.

*She wants us to give newspapers
to a recycling company.*

What other advice did she give? Continue the notes.

4

The manufacturers of Ozo asked Mr and Mrs X's opinion of their new product.
This is what happened. Put the pictures in the right order.

BE GREEN **AND** CLEAN

 Now listen to the advertisement and
check the order of the pictures.

Listen to the advertisement again. Fill in
the missing words in these sentences.
Check your answers with your partner.

1 We asked ... to give ... some articles of clothing.
2 We asked the twins ... shirts.
3 They even ... old washing powder.

Work in groups of three.
Ⓐ **Write down an instruction.**
Ⓑ **Tell C what A wants him/her to do.**
Ⓒ **Do it.**

Example
Ⓐ Open the window.
Ⓑ A wants you to open the window.
Ⓒ (opens the window).

5

Look at these sentences.

1 Mrs X looked at all the shirts. She said she
   was happy with <u>hers</u>.
2 We asked the twins to tell us about their shirts.
   They said they were very pleased with <u>theirs</u>.
3 Then Mr X looked at his shirt. He said <u>his</u>
   was the best.

What do the underlined words refer to?

Now change these sentences using the
possessive pronouns ... *mine, yours, his,*
hers, ours, yours, theirs.

Example
I think my shirt is the best.
I think mine is the best.

1 Your trousers are cleaner.
2 He grows organic vegetables in his garden.
3 Their washing machine is solar-powered.
4 Our washing powder is phosphate-free.

6

The manufacturers of Ozo washing powder have just produced
a new product - Ozo washing-up liquid. They're planning an advertisement
to launch their new product. Look at these notes.

MEMO

To   Date
From

Re: Idea for new ad - Ozo washing-up liquid.

Get two professional dish-washers to test Ozo
washing-up liquid, the new phosphate-free
washing-up liquid. Tell them to bring their
dirtiest plates to challenge Ozo. Get them to
wash half the plates with Liquid Number 1
a well-known brand) and half with Liquid
Number 2 (Ozo). Ask their opinions.
They choose Liquid Number 2 (of course!)
"Wonderful! Definitely!" they say.

Work with a partner. Use the notes in the memo to write out an advertisement in full. Make notes about the pictures you need for your advertisement.

7

Here are three 'renewable energy' products - a solar battery charger, a 'Tutti Fruity' clock and a solar plant turner. Which is which?

Read the descriptions and test results for two of the products. Which two are they?

Now read the texts again and complete this chart.

	clock	battery charger
works in the sun		
works well with potatoes		
takes 14 hours to work		
can work for several days		
is made of plastic		
is not very useful		
has difficult instructions		
may be useful on holiday		

Price £8.99 **What It Is**
A digital display clock
powered by a tiny elec-
trical current generated
by placing electrodes in
any kind of fruit, veget-
able, soft drink - or even
a pot plant. **What we
found** The clock won't
work for very long before
the electrodes need to be
reset; how long it works
depends on what you
place the electrodes in.
Our testers got the best
results with potatoes -
the clock ran for several
days. It will tell you both
the date and the time if it
is set correctly, but many
testers found the instructions for setting the clock
▆▆▆ difficult to follow.
Verdict Fun initially, but
inconvenient for regular
use. Novelty value only.

Price £6.20 **What It Is**
A small plastic box de-
signed to hold four
rechargeable batteries.
The lid contains a small
solar panel that you point
towards the sun. The
manufacturer says that
recharging all four batteries takes up to 14 hours
depending on the
strength of sunshine
and how low the batter-
ies are. **What we found**
We got a reasonable
result in direct strong
sunlight (a table lamp
also gave ▆▆▆ light),
though for the manufac-
turer's charging times
you'd need the stron-
gest summer sunshine.
In heavily overcast con-
ditions recharging the
batteries would take
▆▆▆ long for it to be
practical. **Verdict** May
be useful, perhaps for a
camping holiday. But
▆▆▆ buy this if you
already have a mains
recharger. Mains rechar-
gers are more versatile.

Some words are missing from the texts. Use these words to fill in the gaps.

too   enough   don't

8

Look at the clocks below. What is the difference?

This clock shows you
both the time and the date.

This clock shows you
either the time or the date.

Rewrite these sentences using *both ... and* or *either ... or.*

Example
You can be clean <u>and</u> green.
You can be both clean and green.

1   The battery charger uses the sun <u>or</u> it uses a lamp.
2   The clock works with potatoes <u>and</u> it works with carrots.
3   The batteries can come in a plastic box <u>or</u> in a cardboard box.
4   You must use the positive electrode <u>and</u> the negative electrode.

Study points

You can use the word *work* in
different ways. Look at this sentence.

The clock won't *work* for very long.

This means the clock won't function.

**Look at the following examples
including the word *work* and think
how you say them in your language.**

1   I can't go to the meeting. I've got too
much *work*.
2   This new washing powder *works*
very well.
3   I *work* in the country. I'm an
environmental officer.
4   My plans for the transport campaign
didn't work.
5   She *worked out* how the family could
save energy.

9

 Work in pairs.
Ⓐ **Look at page 115.**

Ⓑ **Look at the instructions below.
Ask questions to find the reason for
each instruction. Begin your questions
like this:**

Why isn't it a good idea to ...?
Why is it important to ...?

Instructions
■ Don't use aerosol sprays.
■ Use a saucepan lid when
you're cooking.
■ Use herb toothpaste.
■ Put tin foil behind radiators.

**Now answer your partner's questions.
Choose the correct answers in the list of
reasons.**

Reasons
□ It uses less water.
□ It saves petrol
and reduces pollution.
□ It's made from trees,
and trees produce oxygen.
□ It's as good as chemicals
and it helps plants to grow.

Grammar and Language

1 Direct and reported commands / requests

a   You can use this form if you give someone a command (or strong request) directly.

> **Don't travel** by car. **Travel** by public transport.

b   If you are reporting instructions/requests, you can do so using verbs like *tell/ want/ ask*. In this way, you show clearly who has given the command/request and who has received/heard it.

I He They	told wanted asked	Mary her you	to	close the window. open the door.

2 Possessive pronouns

You can use a possessive pronoun to show that something belongs to/is connected with someone. It must be clear who and what you are referring to. A possessive pronoun can be the subject or the object of a sentence.

You often use possessive pronouns to contrast things of the same type which belong to different people.

> They all looked at the *shirts*.
>
> *Mrs X* was happy with **hers.**
> *The twins* were pleased with **theirs.**
> *Mr X* said **his** was the best.

3 both ... and, either ... or

a   You can use *and* to link two word groups. If you want to emphasise that you mean both word groups, you put *both* in front of the first word group.

> You can be **both** clean **and** green.

b   You can use *or* to link two word groups. If you want to emphasise the alternatives you put *either* in front of the first word group.

> This clock shows you **either** the time **or** the date.

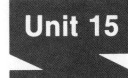
Chance in a million

This month's *City Lights* features you.
We have been finding out what you do, what you like,
what you want out of life.

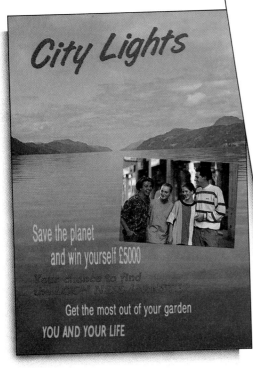

SAVING THE PLANET
WRITE A SHORT STORY AND WIN £5000

We all think we can write a story. This is your chance to prove it. Dust off your typewriter and enter our short story competition now.

The theme of the competition is saving the planet. Your story can be on any subject relating to the environment: pollution; saving energy; recycling; saving the planet.

Your story must be no more than 5000 words and no less than 200 words. Entries must be clearly legible - typewritten on plain white paper.

Closing date for entries is 31st December. The judges will include the editor of *City Lights*, our reporter Susie Harper, leading novelist Nigel Wilder and TV personality Jackie Carr.

We will announce the winners in the March issue of *City Lights* and the winning stories will be printed in the April and May issues. **1st prize** is a fat cheque for £5000; **2nd prize** is £1000; and **10 runners-up** will receive electric typewriters. For a full list of the competition rules and an entry form, see page 87.

Look at the *City Lights* competition feature.

- What must your story be about?
- How long can it be?
- By when do you have to send it to the magazine?
- How many judges will there be?
- What are the prizes?
- Where will you find an entry form?

1

 Listen to these people talking about what they would do if they won the competition.
Match the illustrations with the speakers.

Ask your partner what he/she would do if he/she won. Tell the class.

2

City Lights reporter, Susie Harper, interviewed a lot of people for this month's article on 'You and how you live your life'.

She wanted to find out

- what sports people do.
- who is punctual/late for appointments.
- who can use a computer.
- who is a fast/slow reader and who is a good/bad speller.
- what people would do if they won £1000.
- what people would do if they were ill.

Work in groups. Interview each other.

3

The magazine editor is correcting some sentences from Susie's article.
Choose the correct word or words for each sentence.

1 The most popular sports (was/were) jogging, swimming and cycling.
2 One person said, "If you don't stop asking me questions, I (will/would) be late for a meeting."
3 A lot of people would learn how to use a computer if they (have/had) the time.
4 Most people can read fast but they spell (bad/badly.)
5 "If I won £1000, I (will/would) spend it on flying lessons.", said one woman.
6 Most people would go to the doctor if they (are/were) ill.

4

This month's magazine has a questionnaire. The editor wants to rewrite some of the questions. Complete the new questions.

1 Can you swim well?
   Are you a ...
2 Are you a fast worker?
   Do you ...
3 Are you good at spelling?
   Are you a ...
4 Are you a good gardener?
   Are you interested in ...
5 If you had a lot of time and money, what would you do?
   What would you ...

Now answer the questions.

Complete this table.

verb	noun (a person)
build	builder
travel	
	planner
decorate	
	student
type	
	photographer
advise	
	nurse
garden	

Now write down the name for a person who

- delivers letters
- serves the customers in a restaurant
- drives a taxi
- writes for a newspaper
- works in a library.

5

One of the other articles in *City Lights* this month is about student politics.

Look at this example of a publicity hand-out for a student party.

VOTE FOR THE STUDENTS' REFORM PARTY

If we win this election, we'll change college life!

- We'll build a new library and improve sports facilities.
- We'll appeal for book grants.
- We'll make bus travel free for all students.
- We'll make more accommodation available, and rents will be cheaper.
- We'll make the town a better place to live in. We'll work with conservation groups and plant more trees in the area.

Tom Samuel, Students' Reform Party candidate

Vote for us in this election and you'll help make student life better for all of us!

What do these words mean?
Use your dictionary to help you.

election	party	vote	policy	appeal	reform

Discuss these questions.

- At what age can you vote in your country?
- Do you think young people make good politicians?

Read the students' manifesto. How will the students change student life? Make notes. Use these headings.

grants
library
sports facilities
trees
bus travel
accommodation
rents

Talk to a partner. What do you think of these ideas? How will the student party pay for their reforms?

Work in groups. You are the new students' reform party. Make a list of what you will change. Put your ideas in order of priority and write your manifesto. Present it to the rest of the class.

Now write three sentences about what you would change if you were the director of your school or place of work.

6

Look at this advertisement from *City Lights* for the Gardener's Calendar and the Gardener's Diary. Choose the right words from the list below to complete the advertisement.

Are you interested in ...(1)... your garden for next year? Well, why not get a copy of ...(2)... the Gardener's Calendar or the Gardener's Diary? Or you could buy ...(3)...! The Calendar has 12 stunning photographs and is packed with information to help you get the best from your garden. If you followed the advice in the Gardener's Diary, you ...(4)... a very colourful display for ...(5)... month of the year. There's plenty of advice about how to become an even ...(6)... gardener. There's information about ...(7)... insects and pests, even if you ...(8)... want to use chemicals. Bargain prices: only £2.95 for the Calendar and £3.95 for the Diary. And ...(9)... forget, if you order this month, you get a free address book ...(10)....

1 plan	planing	planning	plans
2 or	both	either	and
3 or	both	either	each
4 would	would have	could	will have
5 all	a	each	the

6 better	good	well	best
7 controlling	controller	control	controling
8 not	no	aren't	don't
9 not	no	aren't	don't
10 both	also	and	too

City Lights is running another competition. Look at the prizes.

Listen to the tape and write down how much each prize is worth.

Work with a partner.

- Put the prizes in order.
- Now ask and answer questions about the prizes.

Example

Ⓐ How much are the books worth?

Ⓑ £500.

Ⓐ Look at page 116.

Ⓑ Look at the information about some of the prizes. Then answer your partner's questions.

The television and video are worth £750 together. They are the latest designs from Japan and come with their own stand. You can choose from white or black. They come with remote controls which are easy to operate.

The English course in Oxford is for one year. You will have free lessons and live with a family in the town. The school is a large one in the centre of Oxford with lots of activities and facilities.

The book prize includes a set of exclusive leather-bound encylopaedias, or you may choose other books to the same value. These can be in any language.

Discuss the prizes.

- Which would you most like to win?
- In each case, would you choose the money or the prize?
- Write reasons for your choices.

Example

I wouldn't choose the car because I can't drive. I would use the money to travel round the world.

8

Congratulations! You have won a week in Scotland monster-hunting. You have looked at the brochures and chosen a hotel you like. You have written to the hotel asking for more information. Complete the letter.

Write a similar letter to a London hotel, booking two nights' accommodation for your shopping trip.

Dear Sir/Madam,

I have won a competition and the prize is a _____ to Loch Ness next summer. I am very interested in the _____ and hope very much to see it!

I am an English student from _____ aged _____. I speak some English but need more practice. I want to come to Scotland in _____ and stay for _____ days.

Could you send me some _____ your _____ and the cost of a _____ about _____ ? I would also like to know about local transport facilities because I will not have a _____.

With many thanks

Yours faithfully

Things used to be different ...

Which pictures show the past and which show the present?

Now find the right picture for each of these captions.

a People used to travel in carriages.
b People used to tell the time by the sun.
c People used to grow most of their own food.
d Horses used to pull ploughs on farms.

What can you say about the other pictures? How is life different today?
Put the pictures in pairs to show past and present.

1

Look at these two pictures of Mary Emsworth.

1940s   1990s

- How has she changed?
- What would you like to know about her?

Make a list of questions.

 Listen to this interview with Mary. Were your questions answered?
Listen again and decide which of these statements are true and which are false.

1 Mary Emsworth used to write short stories when she was a girl.
2 She used to work in a children's hospital.
3 She used to live in London.
4 Life used to be much easier for women.

What can you say about Mary Emsworth's life now in the 1990s?

2

**Complete this passage about Mary Emsworth.
Fill in the gaps with either *used to* or a verb
in the present.**

Today, Mary Emsworth ...... in a small village in the country, but she ...... live in London. Does she miss city life? 'No,' she says, 'not at all. I ...... find city life exciting, but now I ...... the peace of the country.' Mary's life has changed a lot over the years. When she was a young woman, she ...... work in a women's hospital. Nowadays, she ...... a full-time writer and she ...... two books a year!

Now answer these questions on the passage.

1 Did Mary Emsworth use to live in a big city?
2 Did she use to write novels when she was a young woman?

over to you

**Ask a partner about his/her life.
Find out what has changed.**

Example
Where do you live now?
Where did you use to live?

Make notes, then write a short passage about your partner.

3

Work in pairs.
Ⓐ Look at page 115.
Ⓑ Match the pictures with the words in the chart.
Check with your partner.

PRICES IN BRITAIN - TABLE		
	now	20 years ago
loaf of bread	60p	
kilo of sugar		8p
bottle of milk		6p
cup of tea	60p	
litre of petrol		10p
pocket calculator	£12	

Now ask your partner questions to find the
missing information.

Example
How much did a loaf of bread use to cost?
How much does a bottle of milk cost now?

**Complete this summary of the
information in the table.**

PRICES IN BRITAIN - SUMMARY

Twenty years ago, bread, sugar, ... , ..., and
.... used to be cheaper than they are today, but ......
used to be more expensive.

**Make a table for prices in your country and
write a summary. Is it the same as the summary
for Britain?**

Study points

Look at this text and put in the
missing commas, full stops and
capital letters. This information will
help you.

line 1 2 capital letters; 1 full stop
line 2 1 capital letter; 1 comma
line 3 1 comma; 1 full stop; 1 capital letter
line 5 1 full stop

john parker lives in a small seaside town
when he was younger he used to live in the
city but now he enjoys the quiet life' he
spends a lot of time writing and walking
by the sea

Check your answer with a partner.

4

Look at this table. You have three minutes
to add as many things as possible to each column!

cup of tea	bottle of milk	litre of petrol	kilo of sugar

Look at these expressions. Decide which
are like *cup/bottle of* and which are
like *litre/kilo of.*

glass of   pound of
gram of   box of
packet of   can of

Match them with the things in your list.

5

Look at these pictures.

- What do people use these things for?
- Have they got anything in common?

Now read this article and put the pictures in the right historical order.

Money then and now

When you buy something these days, you have so many ways of paying for it. Just think of them! However, you may be surprised to learn that there have always been lots of methods of payment. In very early times, people used to exchange one thing for another - an ox or a cow for rice or grain, for example. This system of exchange was called 'barter', but there were lots of problems. Well, how many heavy bags of rice would <u>you</u> give for a cow ... or a TV, or a car? And how would you carry the bags of rice?

The Ancient Greeks solved these problems. In the 7th century B.C. they introduced coins made of fixed amounts of gold and silver. Business became much easier, because people could now exchange money for things they required.

Coins last a long time, but they are heavy, and so eventually, governments solved the problem by introducing banknotes. So cash became easier and lighter to carry.

Nowadays, of course, more and more people are paying for things with cheques and credit cards instead of in cash. What is the reason for this?

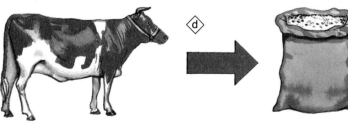

6

Complete this summary about the history of money.

There have always been different ways of paying for things. In......,
people ...... pay for a cow with ...... , for example. Then, in Ancient
Greece, people ...... a system of .... People ..... now buy things
they required ..... money. Because ...... are so heavy,
countries introduced........ . Nowadays, a lot of people
...... for things with ....

Why do so many people use cheques and credit cards today?
Make a list of reasons and compare them with the other students' lists.

7

**Find these words in the text in exercise 5
and make sure you understand them.**

| barter | token | cash | cheque | credit card |

**Now listen to the tape and decide which
of these things the customer is buying
and how he pays for it.**

**Now listen again and put these
expressions into the right order.
Why is the thing too expensive?**

1 How much is it?
2 OK. I'll let you have it for ...
3 Could you give me a receipt, please?
4 I'll take the one with ...
5 That's too expensive.

Match expressions 1-5 with a-e.

a OK. I'll reduce it to ... for you.
b That's too much.
c Can I have a receipt, please?
d What does it cost, please?
e Can I have the one with ... , please?

8

**Look at these objects and decide what
they are. Compare your ideas with
a partner's.**

**What is wrong with these objects? Choose
from these phrases.**

| out-of-date | cracked |
| ripped | dented |

**Work with your partner.
Ⓐ is the customer and wants to buy one of
the objects. He/She must try and persuade
Ⓑ, the shop assistant, to reduce the price.**

9

**Look at these things and decide how you would
pay for them or pay to use them.**

phone call
meal at a restaurant
bus ticket
car
hotel bill

**What is the most useful way of carrying money
with you and paying for things? Why? Compare
your ideas in groups.**

Grammar and Language

1 *used to*

You can use *used to* + infinitive to refer to something that happened regularly/existed in the past but does not happen/exist now. You can also use it to refer to a past state/situation which has changed.

Where did	you she they	**use to**	live? work?

I You She They	**used to** **didn't use to**	live work	in London.

2 Partitives to express amounts

You can specify the amount of something by naming the container/unit/measure followed by *of.*

	cup(s)	**of**	coffee.
	bottle(s)	**of**	milk.
A	**packet(s)**	**of**	sugar.
(Two)	**loaf/(loaves)**	**of**	bread
	litre(s)	**of**	petrol.
	kilo(s)	**of**	sugar.

When and how?

Look at these food items. What are they?

**What are these things made of? How do you think they are made?
Use the words below to help you.**

eggs	milk	sugar	flour	water	cocoa	fruit	butter	cream

**What other ingredients do you think are used?
What ingredient do all these foods have in common?**

1

Look at this advertisement for sugar.

- Which picture shows sugar cane and which picture shows sugar beet?
- One of the words in the headline is used to mean two different things. Which word?

If you thought
sugar was made in manufacturing plants, you were right.

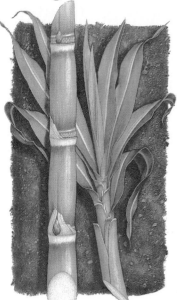

You're looking at two of Nature's sugar factories. On the left, *Saccharum officinarum*, or sugar cane. On the right, *Beta vulgaris*, or sugar beet.

They work every hour daylight sends, seven days a week.

Their raw materials are sunshine, air and water. The finished products are sugars and starches.

Sugar cane was discovered in India more than two thousand years ago.

It grows best in rich soils and humid, tropical climates, so it is planted in countries like Mauritius and the West Indies.

Sugar beet, a large root vegetable, grows well in cool, temparate climates like the English!

Between them these two plants supply most of the world's sugar.

At which point you might fairly ask, if sugar is made by Nature then what on earth do the sugar companies do?

The answer is, we extract, clean and crystallise. We purify sugar for our own use.

A The washed plants are crushed or sliced into hot water, making a dirty brown juice.

This we filter, clean and boil down to a thick syrup, from which pure white sugar can be crystallised.

The dark treacly molasses left behind is used to give brown sugars their characteristic colour and flavour.

And that's it. Brown or white, in plants or packets, sugar is sugar. It contains no colouring. No flavouring. And no preservatives.

Sugar can be extracted from many plants though it seldom makes economic sense.

In Pakistan they use sweet, sticky dates. In the East, cocunut palms. In America, maize. The Canadians take maple syrup from the sap of the maple tree.

Of course, artificial sweeteners are also made in plants. But plants of a rather different kind.

The question is, do you prefer your sweetener made from sodium saccharide, aspartic acid, aceto-acetic acid and phenylalanine?

Or sunshine, air and water?

Sugar. The more you know about it, the sweeter it tastes.

Read the text and complete this chart.

	likes humid tropical climates	likes cool temperate climates	grows in England	grows in the West Indies
sugar cane				
sugar beet				

Check your answers with a partner.

Look at section A of the text.
Make a list of the words you do not understand.
Use a dictionary to find out the meanings.

Now answer the questions about the sugar process.

1 What happens to the washed plants?
2 What is filtered, cleaned and boiled?
3 What gives brown sugar its colour?

2

Look at these sentences about the text and make questions.

Example
Sugar cane is planted in hot countries. *Where is sugar cane planted?*

1 Sugar beet is cultivated in England. *Where ...*
2 The washed plants are crushed and sliced in our factories. *Where ...*
3 The molasses is used to give brown sugars their colour and flavour. *How ...*
4 Pure white sugar is crystallised from the syrup. *What ...*
5 Coconut palms are used for sugar in the East Indies. *Where ...*

3

 Listen to this information about Easter Island and choose the correct information from the alternatives below.

Location	a Atlantic Ocean	b Pacific Ocean	c Mediterranean Sea
Size	a 2,500 sq km	b 1,640 sq km	c 166 sq kms
Population	a 250	b 2,500	c 25,000
Importance	a historical	b medical	c political
Main Products	a fruit & vegetables	b oil	c stone

What is a statue? Use your dictionary to find out.

Read this information about the origin of the stone statues on Easter Island and put these pictures in the right order.

Easter Island is a small island some three thousand kilometres off the coast of Chile in the Pacific Ocean. It is famous for the six hundred stone figures that stand 3 to 12 metres high all over the island.

No one is sure how old the figures are but most people believe they were brought by boat from the South American mainland hundreds of years ago. The gigantic figures were rolled one by one across the island on tree trunks until they reached high ground.

A long wooden pole was put under each figure and the head was lifted off the ground. At the same time, stones were put under the head to stop it falling back. The figure was then lifted again and more stones were put underneath. A rope was also tied around the head, and this was fixed into the ground to stop the figure falling while the stones were put under it. This was repeated until the figure was upright.

All the figures face the sea, and some of them weigh as much as 30 tons. They were not painted or decorated in any way.

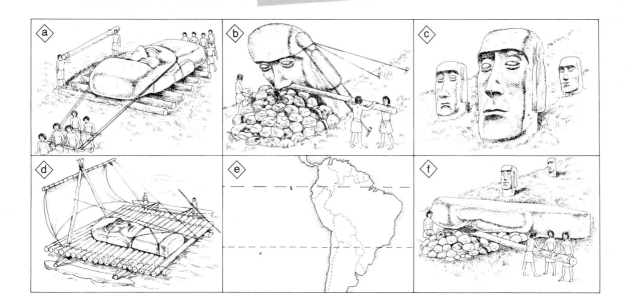

4

Now look back at exercise 3 and answer the questions below about the statues.

1 How old are the figures?
2 How high are the figures?
3 How were the figures brought from South America?
4 What was put under the head to stop it falling back?
5 How heavy are the figures?
6 Were the figures painted?

Look at these sentences about the text. They are wrong. Correct them.

Example
The figures were brought by plane from South America.
The figures were brought by boat.

1 The figures were painted.
2 A rope was tied around the legs.
3 The figures were rolled across the island on wheels.
4 The figures were decorated.
5 Cushions were put under the head to stop it falling back.

5

Do you know the past participles of these verbs?

Example
look - *looked*   put - *put*

1 take	6 produce	11 invent
2 open	7 remember	12 eat
3 study	8 write	13 grow
4 build	9 believe	14 ask
5 make	10 want	15 show

Look at this sentence and how it changes in the passive.

They built the first car in the USA. The first car was built in the USA.

Now change these sentences in the same way.

1 Someone invented the first television in Britain.
2 They grow coffee in Colombia.
3 They produce sugar in the West Indies.
4 Someone took one of the first photographs in France.
5 They showed the first cinema film in 1895.

6

Work in pairs. Look at the pictures below, then make a question for each picture using the question words given.

Example
(Who/write/by?)
Who was Hamlet written by?

1 (When /build?)

2 (When/open?)

3 (Who/write/by?)

4 (When/paint?)

5 (When/build?)

Work in pairs.
Ⓐ **Turn to page 116.**

Ⓐ Turn to page 116.

Ⓑ **Look at the answers below to the questions you have made. Ask your partner for the missing information.**

Hamlet	
Taj Mahal	17th century
Suez Canal	
War and Peace	Leo Tolstoy
Mona Lisa	1503
Eiffel Tower	

Now answer your partner's questions.

7

Look at the three pictures.
What is happening in each picture?

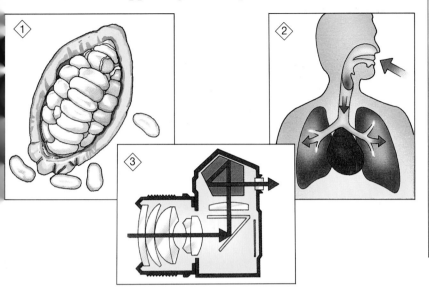

Look at these words and put *a* or *an*
in front of them.

ice cream	vegetable	ocean
statue	trunk	island
bee		

Now listen to these two expressions.

the ocean
the Taj Mahal

**Listen to the pronunciation of *the*
in each case. Why is it different?**

**Now write down the expressions
you hear and put them into two
groups according to the sound of *the*.**

 Listen to three people talking about the processes
and match them with the pictures above. Now listen to the
third process again and fill in the gaps.

The cocoa tree is .... in West Africa. It usually grows to a height of
about 5 to 6 metres. Large pods, about 25cm long, grow on .... tree.
These pods contain about 25-30 cocoa beans. The beans .... taken out
of the pods and .... before they are .... The beans ....
shelled, roasted and then .... into a fine powder. This powder is
.... to make chocolate.

over to you

What processes do you know? What about coffee, bread, wool, cotton?
Work with a partner. Make notes about the stages in the process.
Then explain the process to the class.

8

Divide into three groups. Each group chooses one of the sentences below.
How many different sentences can you make, changing just one part
of the sentence at a time? You have 10 minutes.

Example
1 The statues were brought by boat from South America.
2 The statues were brought by plane from South America.
3 The statues were brought by plane from North America.
4 The statues are brought by plane from North America.
5 .....

Ⓐ The cocoa tree is grown in West Africa.

Ⓑ Some Chinese tea is exported to Europe.

Ⓒ Sugar cane is grown in the West Indies.

**Now compare your final sentence with the original sentence.
Which group produced the most sentences?**

Grammar and Language

The passive

a You can use the passive when you want to emphasise the action rather than the person / thing performing it (the agent).
Here are some possible reasons for choosing the passive.

- You do not know who / what the agent is.
- The agent is not / does not seem important.
- The agent is obvious and therefore does not need a mention.
- You have already mentioned the agent.
- People in general are the agents.

You often use the passive to talk about facts and processes.

	Form of *be*	Subject	Past participle
Where	is was	sugar cane	planted? grown?
How	are were	the figures	lifted? supported?

Subject	Form of *be*	Past participle	
Sugar cane	is was	planted grown	in the West Indies.
Stones	are were	placed put	under the head.

b Sometimes you need to mention the agent. Here are some possible reasons for doing so.

- You want to clarify exactly who / what the agent is.
- You want to refer to the agent in the next sentence.

You can mention the agent using *by* + agent.

Hamlet was written **by Shakespeare.**

Around the world

Look at the information below about eight different countries.
Work with a partner. Put together the correct information for each country.

	A	B	C	D	E	F	G	H
Country								
Capital								
Language								

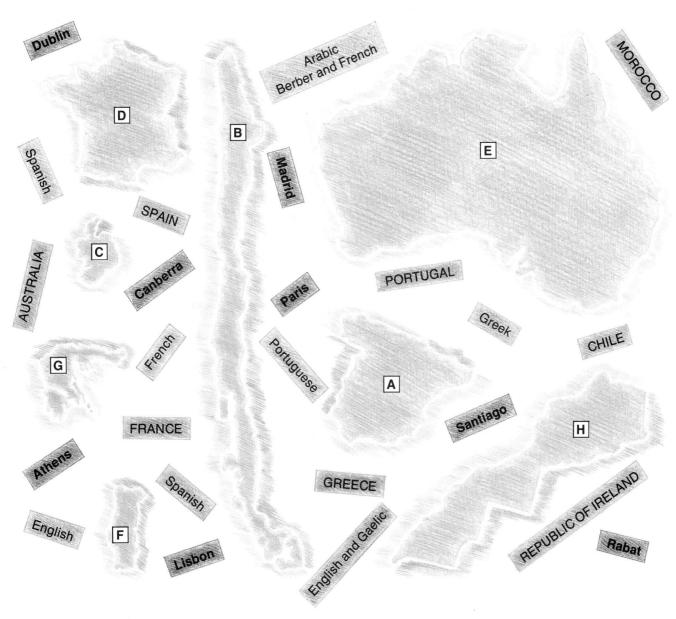

Put the countries in order of size. Which is the biggest and which is the smallest?
Make sentences comparing the countries.

Example
Australia is bigger than Morocco.

1

Look at these islands.

- How big are they?
- How far are they from Venezuela?

Listen to an inhabitant of Trinidad talking about the island. Write down as much information as you can remember about the island.

Now make sentences comparing the following:

Example
Barbados/Trinidad *Trinidad is bigger than Barbados.*

1 Trinidad/Jamaica
2 Barbados/Jamaica
3 population of Trinidad/Barbados
4 climate in Trinidad/Jamaica
5 climate in Barbados/Jamaica

Listen to the tape again and check your sentences.

Make sentences comparing your country with Trinidad.

2

Read the newspaper article below.

- What is it about?
- Can you think of a title?

**Now look at the skyline of buildings.
Read the article again and name the buildings.
Choose from these buildings.**

> Nat West Tower   Empire State Building   Big Ben
> Canary Wharf Tower   Eiffel Tower   Sears Tower

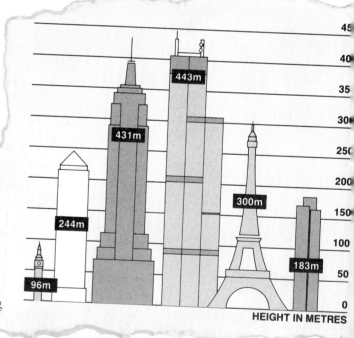

THE CANARY Wharf Tower has soared into almost every view of London's skyline.
Its fifty storeys make it taller than both Big Ben and the Nat West Tower, previously Britain's tallest building. It is not as tall as the Eiffel Tower, however, which remains the tallest building in Europe.
The Empire State Building in New York is taller than all of these, but even this is not as tall as Chicago's Sears Tower, which is the tallest building in the world.

**How tall are the buildings?
Complete the sentences about the buildings.**

1 The Eiffel Tower is not as tall as the ......
2 ...... is not as tall as the Nat West Tower.
3 The Eiffel Tower is not ...... tall ...... the Sears Tower.
4 The Canary Wharf Tower is ...... as tall ...... the Eiffel Tower.

Now work in pairs.

Ⓐ **Close your book.**

Ⓑ **Ask your partner questions to find out how much he/she remembers.**

Example
Is Canary Wharf as big as the Empire State Building?
Is the Empire State Building taller than the Eiffel Tower?

Write sentences comparing the height of buildings in your country.

3

Read the personal profiles below.

Stockbroker

Age: 36

Height: 1.82m

Annual income: £75000

Teacher

Age: 41

Height: 1.5m

Annual income: £12000

Bricklayer

Age: 37

Height: 1.82m

Annual income: £16000

Doctor

Age: 29

Height: 1.6m

Annual income: £24000

Now look at these sentences. Some of them are wrong. Correct them.

1 The teacher isn't as tall as the doctor.
2 The doctor is older than the stockbroker.
3 The bricklayer is younger than the doctor and the teacher.
4 The doctor is shorter than the teacher.
5 The stockbroker is probably richer than the doctor and me!
6 The stockbroker is wealthier than the bricklayer.

Now rewrite the sentences using pronouns.

Example
The teacher isn't as tall as the doctor. She isn't as tall as her.

4

Look at this graph. What sort of information does it give? Use your dictionary to help you.

	B	DK	D	GR	E	F	IRL	I	L	NL	P	UK
Demography												
Total population (x 1 000)	9 870	5 127	61 199	9 990	38 832	55 630	3 543	57 345	372	14 665	10 250	56 930
percentage of men	48.8	49.3	47.9	49.2	49.1	48.7	50.0	48.6	48.6	49.4	48.3	48.7
percentage of women	51.2	50.7	52.1	50.8	50.9	51.3	50.0	51.4	51.4	50.6	51.7	51.3
percentage aged under 20	25.7	25.5	22.5	28.2	31.1	28.7	38.3	26.9	24.0	26.5	31.4	26.9
percentage aged over 60	19.9	20.4	20.5	18.4	17.2	18.4	14.8	18.9	18.3	17.4	17.3	20.7
Estimated population in 2010 (x 1 000)	9 433	5 044	58 587	10 335	41 194	58 760	3 417	56 411	377	16 103	11 114	59 375
Number of households (1 000)	3 716	2 892	26 352	3 234	10 793	20 906	1 007	20 118	134	5 439	3 099	21 816
Average number of persons per household	2.7	1.8	2.3	3.1	3.6	2.7	3.5	2.9	2.8	2.7	3.3	2.6
Birth rate (per 1 000)	11.9	11.0	10.5	10.7	11.2	13.8	16.6	9.6	11.4	12.7	12.0	13.6
Life expectancy at birth (years)												
men	70.0	71.6	71.2	72.2	72.5	71.5	70.1	71.4	70.0	72.9	70.3	71.6
women	76.8	77.5	77.8	76.4	78.6	79.7	75.6	78.1	76.7	79.7	77.1	77.5
Marriages (per 1 000 inhabitants)	5.7	6.1	6.3	6.6	5.3	4.7	5.1	5.3	5.3	6.0	7.0	7.0
Divorces (per 1 000)	2.0	2.8	2.1	0.9	0.5	2.0	—	0.5	2.0	1.9	0.9	2.9
Mortality (per 1 000)	10.7	11.3	11.2	9.6	7.9	9.5	8.8	9.3	10.8	8.3	9.3	11.3
Infant mortality (per 1 000)	9.7	8.3	8.3	11.7	8.8	7.8	7.4	9.6	9.4	7.6	14.2	9.1

NB - See note on Germany on page ii

Work with a partner. Use the graph to answer these questions.

1 Which European countries do the flags represent?
2 Which country has the largest population?
3 Which country has the highest proportion of people over 60?
4 Which countries have an increasing population?
5 Who can expect to live longer - men or women?
6 Where is divorce illegal?
7 Which country has the highest mortality rate?

5

Read these sentences and say whether they are true or false using the information in the graph.

1 Italy has the same number of divorces as Spain.
2 More babies die in Ireland than in France.
3 In Greece there are more marriages than in Portugal.
4 There are the same number of marriages in Spain as in Italy.

Look at these nouns. Are they countable or uncountable?

> baby   rain   unemployment   household

You use *fewer* with countable nouns and *less* with uncountable nouns. Complete these sentences with *fewer* or *less*.

1 ...... babies are born in Italy than in Belgium.
2 There is .... unemployment in Luxembourg than in any other EC country.
3 There are ...... households in Greece than in Spain.
4 There is ...... rain in southern Europe than in northern Europe.

Now write four sentences yourself using *fewer* and *less*.

over to you

Write sentences comparing your country with one of the countries in the table. Use *more...than, the same... as, fewer...than* or *less...than*. Exchange your sentences with another student's and say whether you think his/her sentences are true or false.

6

Joanna van Klett is a statistician. She works at the EC headquarters.

Look back at the graph in exercise 2. You will hear Joanna talking about the number of people aged under 20, life expectancy, marriage and divorce. Listen and note down what she says about each of these topics.

Irl - about 38% of population under 20
DK - about 25% of population under 20

Listen again and check your notes. Now write your notes as full sentences, summarising the comparisons Joanna makes.

There are more people under 20 in Ireland than in Denmark.

7

Work in pairs.
Ⓐ Look at page 117.
Ⓑ Look at this information about rivers.

GANGES   AMAZON   LIMPOPO

Compare the lengths of the three rivers so that your partner can identify them.

Example
The Limpopo is not as long as the Ganges.

Now your partner will tell you about the comparative temperatures in Mexico City, London, Cairo and Edinburgh. Use the information to complete the chart.

countries				
temperatures	11°C	11°C	25°C	32°C

8

Look at the text.
- Which country is it about?
- What type of text is it?

Look at these words and, in pairs, decide which things would be useful on an expedition to Iceland. Use a dictionary.

> swimsuit crampons ice axe
> tent sleeping bag torch book
> warm clothes binoculars

Now read the text and see if you were right.

Why were the things listed above useful? Give a reason for each object.

Now in groups decide what you would take on a holiday to Trinidad.

Agree on the five most important things. Compare your list with other groups'.

Iceland offers some of the world's most magnificent unspoilt scenery.

With low temperatures even in summer, and extremely cold winds coming off the glaciers, you will need to pack your winter woollies!

But don't forget your swimsuit, for, strange as it seems, open-air swimming is one of the major attractions. Volcanic springs create warm lakes even when there is snow on the ground.

There are very few towns in Iceland and only a small number of hotels and hostels, so camping is the ideal way to get close to the glaciers. A decent tent and a really strong sleeping bag will give you the freedom you need to see the real glory of Iceland.

If you intend to explore the glaciers, crampons are a must, and an ice axe would be extremely helpful! Birdwatchers - remember your binoculars! You'll be disappointed if you miss Iceland's rare Arctic birds.

In winter, the nights can be very long and the days quite short, so plan your trips carefully and take a torch and a good book!

Study points

Look at this list of nouns. Complete the chart with the corresponding adjective for each one.

Noun	Adjective
death	dead
cold	
heat	
hunger	
wealth	
length	

Now complete these sentences with an appropriate noun or adjective from the list.
1. The Limpopo River isn't as ... as the River Ganges.
2. Iceland isn't as ... as Egypt.
3. Bangladesh is not as ... as Japan.
4. The desert can be extremely ... at night.

9

Find these adverbs in the text in exercise 8.

> extremely very quite

Which is the strongest/weakest? Now use your dictionary to find the meaning of these adverbs.

> really fairly highly

Match them with the adverbs above.

Write about the list of items you chose to take on your holiday in exercise 8 using the adverbs.

Example
I think a ...... would be really important because ..

Grammar and Language

1 Making comparisons

a When you want to describe the difference in a quality between two things / people, you can use a comparative adjective + *than* with a noun or object pronoun.

| The teacher is | **taller**
more experienced | **than** | the doctor.
her. |

b When you want to describe the similarity in a quality between two things, you can use *as* + adjective + *as*.

| The teacher is just **as** | **tall**
experienced | **as** | the doctor.
her. |

c When you want to describe differences in quantity, you can use *more... than, less/fewer... than* (*less* + uncountable noun, *fewer* + plural countable noun).

| There | is | **more/less** unemployment | here **than** there. |
| | are | **more/fewer** households | |

d When you want to describe similarity in numbers, you can use *the same number of... as*.

There are **the same number of** marriages here **as** there.

2 Adverbs of degree

You can give more information about an adjective by using an adverb of degree before it.

| There are | **extremely**
very
quite | cold winds in winter. |

Eastern promise

Look at the picture. These people are on holiday in Nepal.
What can you say about the people and the place?

What kind of occasion is it? What do you think the people are saying?

1

Listen to one conversation on tape. Turn back to page 103 and decide who is talking.
Now listen again. Which of these adjectives apply to Nepal?

> flat small mountainous large fertile
> landlocked green coastal peaceful noisy

Which apply to your country?

Now complete the text about Nepal.
Use the map and the appropriate words above to help you.

Nepal is a ..... , ... kingdom in the Himalayas. It lies ..... India and China with a population of approx- imately 16,000,000. Nepal's capital city is Kathmandu and the national currency is the rupee. Nepali is the main language.

Nepal is a very..... country, particularly in the ..... and is home to Mount Everest, the world's highest mountain.

In the ..... of the country, there are some high, ... valleys which produce rice, maize, millet and wheat.

It is a popular destination for tourists who enjoy walking in the ..... foothills of the Himalayas.

CHINA

NEPAL

Mount Everest

BHUTAN

INDIA

BANGLADESH

2

Listen to the first conversation again and two more conversations.
Complete each sentence with the right question tag from the box.

1 You've been here before, ...
2 It's so green, ...
3 You can't see Everest from here, ...
4 You certainly need warm clothing, ...
5 You're leaving tomorrow, ...
6 It doesn't take long to get used to the outdoor life, ...
7 You won't forget to ring me, ...

> aren't you?
> isn't it?
> can you?
> will you?
> haven't you?
> does it?
> don't you?

Try to complete these sentences with the right question tag, then listen and check.

> have you? is it? aren't you can't you?

1 You're from Australia, ...
2 You haven't been to Nepal before, ...
3 You can see for miles, ...

3

Look at the text in exercise 1 again and correct the information in this table.

Name of country: Nepal
Location: between China and Tibet
Capital city: Lhasa
Main language: Chinese
Currency: chetrum
Population: 12,000,000
Landscape: flat
Crops: barley, oats

Work with a partner and ask questions to check that you have the same information.

Example
It isn't between China and Tibet, is it?
It's between India and China, isn't it?

over to you

Write about a country you know using the text in exercise 1 as a model. Read the text to your partner. Ask him/her to put the information in a table like the one above.

Now your partner will ask you questions to check that he/she has written down the right information.

Example
The country is Spain, isn't it?

4

Can you complete these exchanges from the last conversation? Listen again if you need to.

Man: You ..... from Australia, ... you.
Woman: Yes, that's right.
Man: Well, so am I!

Man: You ..... been to Nepal before, ... you?
Woman: No, never.
Man: Neither have I. But I' ..... certainly come back again sometime.
Woman: Oh, so will I! I've really enjoyed it.

Now complete these dialogues. Choose the correct expressions from the box.

So do I.   So am I.   Neither have I.   Neither can I.   Neither will I.

5

Why do people go on holiday? Look at these reasons. Which do you think are most important? Put them in order.

cultural activities

meeting people

sightseeing

good food

a good social life

sunshine and fresh air

peace and quiet

relaxation

lots of exercise and outdoor activities

Work with a partner. Ask questions to find out what is important for him/her. Then tell him/her what you think.

Example
Are you interested in sightseeing?
No, not really.
Neither am I./ Oh, I love it.

6

Take a closer look at the food from the party on page 103. What can you identify?

Group the items under these headings.

lots of	a few	a little
eggs	tomatoes	tea

7

Put the words in the right order to make expressions for offering these things. Now listen to the extracts on the tape to check.

1 you/like/orange juice/would/more/some?
   - Oh, no thanks. I've had enough already.

2 you/get/me/some/orange juice/let.
   - Oh, thank you. I'd love some.

3 you/get/I /can/tea/some?
   - Oh, thank you. That would be lovely.

Work with a partner. Find out what your partner's likes and dislikes are! Offer him/her some of the things on the table.

8

Listen to these people at a party playing the 'Yes/No' party game.

The player has to answer the questions without saying 'yes' or 'no'. Write down the expressions he uses instead.

Example
That's right.

Now it's your turn. Work with a partner.

Ask questions to check information about your partner. Your partner must answer without using 'yes' or 'no'.

Study points

Look at this page from a dictionary. The headword at the top left (efficiency) shows the first headword on the page. The word in the top right (egg) shows the last headword.

All the headwords in between are in alphabetical order. Which of these words would you find on this page of the dictionary?

eight   efficient   Eastern   either   effort   eggcup   effortless   e.g.   effective   egalitarian

Now use your dictionary to find the words below and write down their first meaning as quickly as possible.

accept   few   get   holiday   much   little   promise   travel

Grammar and Language

1 Question tags

You can add a question tag to a statement when you think you are right about something but you want to check/make sure.

When the statement is affirmative, the question tag is negative; when the statement is negative, the question tag is affirmative.

The subject of the question tag is always a personal pronoun and it relates to the subject in the statement. The verb in the question tag is an auxiliary or a form of *be* or *do*.

Statement	Question tag
Subject + Verb	Auxiliary / *be* / *do* + Subject

You **haven't** been here before,	**have** *you*?
*They***'ll** come back,	**won't** *they*?
It's a lovely place,	**isn't** *it*?
You **can** see it's mountainous,	**can't** *you*?
They **don't** want to leave yet,	**do** *they*?
Tom **wants** to return,	**doesn't** *he*?

You can answer tag questions with short answers.

It's a lovely place, **isn't** *it*?	Yes, *it* **is**.

2 So... / Neither...

You can use *so* / *neither* + auxiliary / *be*/ *do* to respond to statements and express similar states, actions or opinions relating to someone/something else. You use *So* . . . in response to an affirmative statement and *Neither* . . . in response to a negative statement.

Statement		Response
Helen's been here before.	→	**So have** we.
Nepal **is** very mountainous.	→	**So is** Tibet.
Jim **likes** walking.	→	**So do** Helen and Steve.

Jim **hasn't** been here before.	→	**Neither have** I.
Nepal **isn't** a flat country.	→	**Neither is** Tibet.
Helen **doesn't** want to leave.	→	**Neither do** we.

3 Determiners: *a little* / *a few*

If you want to talk about a small amount of something, you can use *a little* with an uncountable noun.

If you want to talk about a small number of things, you can use *a few* with a plural countable noun.

There	is **a little**	orange juice tea	left.
	are **a few**	tomatoes eggs	

A matter of taste

Look at this month's cover of *City Lights*.

- What is the main feature about?
- What else can you read about in this issue?

5th BIRTHDAY celebrations!

Food around the world

The power of chocolate

Stately Weekends

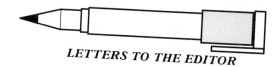

LETTERS TO THE EDITOR

What an interesting article about travel in your recent issue! I disagree with one thing you said, however. Travelling by sea to France is not always a relaxing way to start your holiday. If the sea is rough, you can look forward to five hours of misery!

With people being sick, children screaming, and feeling like death yourself, I'd rather fly or take the train through the Tunnel any day!

Ms L Hutton, Leeds.

Congratulations on your First Aid campaign! I do agree that everyone should be taught first aid, so that they know what to do in an emergency.

Your article helped save my neighbour's life! I was round at her house helping her fill in some forms, when she suddenly collapsed. I didn't panic. I followed your advice and the ambulance was there in minutes.

Now she's fine again. Thanks to your article, I knew exactly what to do.

Bob Trees, Belfast.

So much for your article on the efficiency of the transport system! I recently travelled from my home in London to a friend's in Bristol - a simple journey which should take three hours, at most, door to door. It took six hours. No, there was no blizzard! No, there was no rail strike!

First I had to wait half an hour for a bus, then the bus that finally came broke down. Of course, I missed my train. The next one was cancelled, and the one I finally caught stopped at every station on the way.

When I finally got there, there were no taxis or buses, so I had to walk. No wonder people use their cars instead of public transport! I shall too, in future.

Janet Jones, London.

Look at the letters to the editor and answer these questions as quickly as you can.

- What is each letter about?
- Which letter agrees with the magazine?
- Who does not like travelling by sea?
- Who is complaining about public transport?
- Who saved a neighbour's life?

1

City Lights reporter, Susie Harper, interviewed a chef at a top London restaurant for this month's article on food and entertainment.

She wanted to find out
- where he used to work
- what his speciality is
- when the restaurant kitchens were modernised
- the prices of some of the dishes on the menu
- what his favourite dish is and how it is made

Work in pairs and act out the interview. One of you is Susie, the other is André, the chef.

 Now listen to the interview and note down André's answers. Compare his answers with your's.

What did Susie invite André to do?

2

The magazine editor is correcting some sentences from Susie's article.
Choose the correct word or words for each sentence.

1 People used to (eat/eating) more cream than they do now.
2 These days most customers (use/used) credit cards to pay for their meals.
3 The tea we serve in our restaurant is (growed/grown) in the hills of Sri Lanka.
4 Most people find that if they drink (too much/too many) coffee in the evening, they can't sleep.
5 The new Spanish restaurant in town has (a/the) wonderful menu.

3

Now the editor wants to rewrite some of the sentences in the article.
Complete the new sentences.

1 There were more tourists eating at London restaurants last year.
 This year ...
2 Maxime's Restaurant is not as famous as L'Estrelle.
 L'Estrelle is ...
3 Cleandra opened her first restaurant, L'Estrelle, in 1953.
 L'Estrelle ...
4 The lobster is more expensive than the trout.
 The trout is ...
5 André said he loves eating out. Well, me too.
 André said he loves eating out. Well, so ...
6 I think you've tried the fish dish.
 You've tried the fish dish, ...?

4

Look at the illustration from an article in the *City Lights* food feature.
What do you think it's about? Talk to a partner. Discuss these questions.

- Do you like chocolate?
- How often do you eat it?
- Why do you eat it?

Now read this extract from the article.

Everyone knows that potatoes came from the Americas, but did you know that chocolate first came from the New World too?

It was found there by Christopher Columbus. He brought some cocoa beans back to Spain. At first, however, nobody was interested in them. People thought they were useless.

Later, it was Cortes, the explorer, who tasted the drink in Mexico and brought it back to the Spanish king in 1521.

In Mexico chocolate, or *xocolatl*, was a strong bitter drink with very great powers. It was used in ceremonies for the gods, used at births and at funerals and given to brave soldiers. One Spanish soldier wrote, "It is a marvellous strong drink which helps a man to walk one whole day without other food."

In Spain, the new drink soon became very fashionable, but there they added sugar and vanilla (both of these also recently imported from the New World) and made the drink we know today.

Use your dictionary to find these words.

useless   strong   bitter   whole

Discuss the answers to these questions about chocolate. Write notes.

- Where was it found?
- Who was it found by?
- Where was it brought to?
- How was it used in Mexico?
- What did the Mexican drink taste like?
- What was added in Spain?

Now use your notes to write a summary of the article.

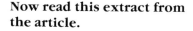
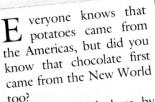

Chocolate was first found in the Americas by

5

City Lights did a questionnaire on healthy eating. Here are one person's answers.

Work with a partner.
Can you work out the questions?

Questionnaire on Healthy Eating	
Questions	**Answers**
What did you have for breakfast?	Tea, toast and marmalade
	Cheese
	Too many
	No, I often miss it
	About 64 kilos
	Sometimes, mainly in Chinese restaurants
	Only easy things like omelettes
	No, it keeps me awake at night

Now change partners. Ask your questions.
Then answer your new partner's questions with your own opinions.

Study points

Can you change these words to make their meanings opposite?
Add *un-*, *in-*, or *im-* to the beginning or change the ending to *-ful* or *-less*.
Use your dictionary if you need help.

Example useless - useful

1	careful	5	pleasant
2	kind	6	selfish
3	fashionable	7	helpful
4	efficient	8	possible

6

One of the other articles in this month's *City Lights* is called 'Weekends Away'.
It talks about stately homes to visit in Britain.

Look at these pictures.

- What are 'stately homes'?
- Do you know any of these houses?
- When do you think they were built?

Work in pairs and discuss what you think life used to be like in the homes.
Use these words to help you.

| rich poor servants tax public balls |
| gardens amusement park paintings |

Now listen to the tape and make notes about

- what life used to be like
- what life is like now.

Compare your notes in pairs. Listen again and check your answers.

7

Now look at the information in these brochure extracts about Longleat and Beaulieu.

" A Beaulieu-full day for everyone! "

Whether you're driving or travelling by public transport you'll love the journey through the beautiful New Forest. Inclusive admission (£6.00 adult, £4.50 child) covers the National Motor Museum, Palace House and beautiful Beaulieu Abbey with its exhibition of monastic life. Plus vouchers for a choice of special features: model car and bike rides for the children to enjoy; a live motoring show and a trip on the Monorail - travelling through the grounds of this magnificent stately home at high level - a great way to see Beaulieu!

Lions of Longleat

Experience the excitement of the African Savannah ... in rural England! Forget about the expense of a trip to Africa. Longleat has it all: lions, gorillas, zebras, monkeys, rhinos and the only white tigers in Britain - and right on your doorstep! If you prefer peace and quiet, take a walk through the butterfly garden. Children! You'll be amazed by our maze and other attractions. The price for all this - just £9.50 (children and senior citizens £7.50) inclusive - great value!

Work with a partner.

- What can you do there?
- What would you like to see?

Now write sentences comparing Longleat and Beaulieu. Which is more interesting, more expensive, more unusual?

8

Work in groups and make plans for *City Lights'* fifth birthday party. Do not let the other groups hear what you are deciding.

Group A Decide on the number of guests, the place, the time.
Group B Make a list of what food to get and how much.
Group C Make a list of what drinks to get and how much.
Group D Decide on the music, decorations and entertainment.

Discuss your plans with the other groups. What sort of party will it be?

- Have you planned enough food?
- Have you planned too much drink?
- Have you got the right sort of music?
- Have you got enough decorations?

9

 Here are two conversations overheard at the party. Complete them by choosing the correct responses a-h.

Conversation 1

- Hello. Are you enjoying yourself?
-
- Yes, of course. What would you like?
-
- Have you had anything to eat yet?
-
- What are you doing these days?
-
- Are you going away?
-
- Oh, how lovely! Have a good trip!

Conversation 2

- Would you like a sandwich?
-
- There's more than enough food. We got far too much!
-
- No, only half the guests have come.
-
- Yes, that's okay though, isn't it?

(a) Yes, we're going to spend a few days in the country.
(b) Yes, thanks. I've had too much. It was marvellous.
(c) Does than mean there's too much to drink, too?
(d) Yes, thank you. Can I have another drink, please?
(e) Is everyone here?
(f) Just an orange juice, please.
(g) Yes, please, I'm really hungry.
(h) Oh, I'm working at a new school in the town, but we're on holiday at the moment.

Now listen to the tape and check.

Pairwork

Unit 2   Exercise 4

A You have just arrived at the airport.
Imagine you have the following problems.
Tell your partner. He/She will make suggestions.

- I've got so much luggage. How am I going to manage?
- I need to change these traveller's cheques.
- My purse has been stolen!
- I've lost my passport.
- I really need a coffee.

Unit 3   Exercise 10

A Read the texts and complete the chart below.
Then answer your partner's questions
about the Shilton International.

	Location	Opening hours	Telephone numbers
post office			
bank			
bookshop			
cafeteria			
travel agent's			
newsagent's			

Now ask your partner questions to
complete your chart.
Turn back to page 17 and complete the rest of the exercise.

SHOPPING AT THE SHILTON

Post Office

Our post office, on the ground floor, offers full postal facilities. It is open from Monday - Friday, 9.00 - 17.00, and on Saturday, 9.30 - 13.00. Tel: 2512922

Bookshop

We have a wide range of books and magazines in many different languages. You'll find us on the ground floor and we are open every day of the week, except Sunday, from 9.30 a.m. to 5.30 p.m. For specific information, please contact us on 2912245.

Newsagent's

You'll find the newsagent's on the ground floor near the main entrance. Open daily from 8 a.m. - 6p.m. We have a wide selection of international newspapers and maps. We are always happy to place any special orders for newspapers which we do not stock. For further information please call 2922338.

Unit 5   Exercise 6

A Look at the information
from *City Lights* about visiting
the UK and ask your partner
the following questions:

1   Do I need a visa to go to the UK?
2   Are hotels expensive in London?
3   Can I use a credit card in the UK?
4   Where can I change travellers cheques?
5   Can I hire a bicycle?

Now answer your partner's questions.

Electricity The standard voltage is 220-240V AC. Power sockets take plugs with three square pins. Fuses are three, five and thirteen amps. Visitors from overseas bringing their own electrical appliances may need an adaptor (available from airport shops, and most shops selling electrical goods).

Currency The pound sterling (£) is worth 100 pence. Silver coins are 5p, 10p, 20p and 50p. Copper coins are 1p and 2p. The only gold-coloured coin is the £1 coin. Notes are £5, £10, £20, £50 and £100. See Banks, Traveller's Cheques and Credit Cards.

Driving You can drive in Britain with a valid International Driving Permit or a driving licence from your country of origin. The minimum age for driving a car is 17. Drive on the left and overtake on the right. The speed limit in residential areas is 30 mph (48kph), 70mph (112kph) on motorways and dual carriageways and 60mph (96kph) on other roads (unless otherwise indicated).

Airports Heathrow (26km west of the city) is the main London terminus (tel: 081 759 2525 for flight information). It is linked to the city centre by underground railway (Piccadilly Line). Trains run from 05.30 to midnight, leave every four to eight minutes, and the journey takes about 45 min. London Transport operates a 24-hour express Airbus to the centre which takes from 30 min. to over an hour depending on the traffic. Airbus services usually terminate at Victoria Coach Station. There is also an all-night bus service (N97) between Heathrow and Trafalgar Square. A taxi will take about 45 min. but can cost up to £20. London's other main airport is Gatwick (42km south of the city).

Customs:

Duty Paid Into:	Cigarettes	or	Cigars	or	Tobacco	Spirits	Wine
E.E.C.	300		75		400 g	1.5 l	5 l
U.K.	300		75		400 g	1.5 l	5 l

Unit 6   Exercise 4

Ⓐ Look at the customer survey again and use the information to answer your partner's questions.

Now ask your partner questions to complete your survey.

Example
How many customers wear special clothes to work?

What colours do eleven of the customers prefer?

CUSTOMER SURVEY Questions	Answers	Customers
1 What kind of clothes do you usually wear for work?	Smart clothes	19
	Special clothes (e.g. uniform)	70
2 What kinds of fibres do you prefer?	Synthetic fibres	50
	Natural fibres	40
	Mixed fibres	10
3 What colours do you prefer?	Dark colours	11
		22
	A mixture of light and dark colours	67
4 Do you feel unhappy about wearing leather or fur?	Yes	5
	No	83
5 How do you wash your clothes?		17
		0
	By hand	57
6 What feature do you look for in particular when you are choosing new clothes?	Comfort	11
	Style	15
	Usefulness	17
	Quality	

Unit 7   Exercise 2

Ⓐ Look at this picture of an area in England five years ago. Make a note of its features under these headings.

location	buildings	transport

Ask your partner questions to find out what it is like now five years later. Make notes.

Example
Ⓐ Is there a bus service?
Ⓑ Yes, there is.

Now answer your partner's questions about the area five years ago.

Example
Ⓑ Were there any houses?
Ⓐ Yes, there were.

Ⓑ Where there any bungalows?
Ⓐ No, there weren't.

Now look at page 37.
Do you recognise the area?

Unit 11   Exercise 5

ⒶLook at the chart and ask your partner questions to find the missing information.

Example
Is she good at ...?
Does she enjoy...?

		good at ...	likes ...				enjoys ...	
Y = yes N = no		spelling	typing	working in an office	writing letters	talking to people	swimming	playing tennis
1	Kenneth Brown	N	Y	Y		Y	Y	N
2	Diane Perry	N	N	N	Y	Y		
3	.... Parker		Y	Y	Y			N

Now answer your partner's questions.

Write about person number 3. Check to see if you and your partner have written the same. Now turn to page 59 and complete the rest of the exercise.

Unit 12   Exercise 3

Ⓐ Study this plan for the Hanging Gardens Hotel and Conference Centre. Then answer your partner's questions.

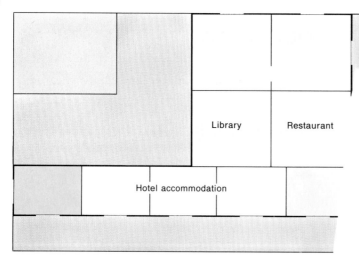

Hanging Gardens Centre PLAN 1

Library   Restaurant

Hotel accommodation

Hanging Gardens Hotel and Conference Centre
● *planning information* ●

Location: inland, 30km from coast and nearest major town

Climate: mainly dry, not much rain

Average temperatures: summer 22°C winter 10°C

Purpose of Centre: to provide hotel accommodation and conference facilities for up to 500 people

Now ask your partner questions to find the missing information on your plan.

Turn back to page 64 and complete the exercise.

Unit 14   Exercise 9

ⒶAnswer your partner's questions. Choose the correct answers from the list of reasons.

Reasons
☐ 1 It saves energy because the food boils faster.
☐ 2 It reflects heat back into the room.
☐ 3 They destroy the ozone layer.
☐ 4 It doesn't contain any unnecessary chemicals.

Now look at the instructions below. Ask questions to find the reason for each instruction. Begin your questions like this:

Why isn't it a good idea to...?
Why is it important to...?

Instructions
■ Use public transport.
■ Water the garden with cold tea.
■ Take a shower instead of a bath.
■ Don't waste paper.

Unit 15   Exercise 7

Ⓐ Ask your partner the following questions about some of the prizes.

Where are the TV and video made?
What colour are they?
Do they have remote control?
Where is the English course?
How long is the course?
What are the books like?
What language are the books in?

Now look back at page 84 and complete the rest of the exercise.

Unit 16   Exercise 3

Help your partner match the pictures with the words in the chart.

Use the information below to answer your partner's questions.

PRICES IN BRITAIN - TABLE		
	now	20 years ago
loaf of bread		5p
kilo of sugar	59p	
bottle of milk	30p	
cup of tea		10p
litre of petrol	50p	
pocket calculator		£20

Now ask your partner questions to find the missing information in your chart.

Unit 17   Exercise 7

Ⓐ Use the information in the table below to answer your partner's questions.

Hamlet	Shakespeare
Taj Mahal	
Suez Canal	1869
War and Peace	
Mona Lisa	
Eiffel Tower	1889

Now ask your partner for the information you need to complete your table.

Unit 18   Exercise 9

Ⓐ Look at these three rivers.
Your partner will tell you about their comparative lengths. Which is which?

2507Km   6440Km   1770Km

Compare these September temperatures for your partner.

countries	Edinburgh	London	Mexico City	Cairo
temperatures	☼	☼	☼	☼

Example Cairo is hotter than Mexico City.

Wordlist

Words in bold type represent the core vocabulary for *Take 2* and are based on a corpus of the most frequently used words in English. Normal type indicates that the word is receptive. Figures refer to page numbers where a word is first introduced. Where more than one page number is given, this indicates that the word is featured with more than one meaning, or that the word is first introduced receptively.

electric 76
electrode 78
embassy 27
emergency 53
employee 64
empty 50
encyclopaedia 84
energy 22, 75
enormously 43
enough 20
enter 81
envelope 77
environment 75
estimate 43
exactly 61
exciting 71
excuse 38
executive 60
exercise 44, 71
expectancy 99
expedition 101
expense 112
explore 101
extent 22
extra 76
extract 92
extremely 15, 101
eyesight 20

fabulous 3
facility 17
factory 72
fairly 101
farm 85
farmer 57
fascinating 15
fashion 15
favourite 33
fax 15
feature 26
fertile 104
few 30, 106
fibre 31
field 55
figure 93
filter 92
fine 95
fire 69
fish 41, 69
fit 20
fix 93
flat 104
flavour 92
flight 55
fluently 60
foggy 67
foreign 60
formal 38
fountain 28

foyer 14
freedom 101
frequent 66
fresh 43
frightening 49
front door 35
frosty 67
fry 42
full-time 72
fully-fitted 36
funeral 110
fur 31
furnished 9

Gaelic 97
garage 35
gardener 82
gardening 42
gate 35
ghostly 50
gigantic 93
glacier 101
glass 75
gloomy 49
gorilla 112
government 28
grain 88
gram 87
grant 83
great 36
grind 42
ground hostess 8
ground 93
grow up 21
grow 92
guarantee 66
guest 9
gun 54

hairdresser's 14
hairspray 75
half 30
hammer 70
handle 50
harm 75
harmful 75
heart 36
heating 76
heliport 66
helpful 101
herb 43
hi 1
highly 101
holiday 103
home 35
hometown 1
hormone 22

hospitality 11
hostel 26
hostess 8
household 99
housewarming 38
housing 22
however 22
humid 92
hunt 69
hurry 50

ice axe 101
Iceland 101
ideal 11
identity 27
immigration 8
impossible 36
improve 64
in common 2
inclusive 112
income 30
increase 43
independent 22
indoors 41
infant 99
ingredient 43
inhabitant 98
inland 64
insect 83
instead of 77
interpreter 60
into 14
introduce 3
invent 94
invitation 38
invite 38
island 11, 70
issue 81

Jamaica 98
Japanese 60
jogging 82
journey 112
judge 81
juice 92

key 16
kingdom 104
knock over 48

ladder 48
lamp 79
landlocked 104
land 55
landscape 105

language 29
launch 78
launderette 31
layer 43
lead 50
length 100
let 9
lid 79
lifestyle 41
lift 14
light 31, 76
likely 71
lion 28
litre 87
little 30
loaf 87
lobster 110
located 17
location 36
lonely 3
lovely 15
low 101
lucky 60
luxurious 15

machine 57
maize 104
manage 57
manifesto 83
manufacturer 77
marmalade 111
market 15
marriage 99
match 70
maximum 65
maze 112
media 33
message 5
middle-aged 19
mild 67
millet 104
ministry 28
mirror 70
misery 109
miss 86
mixed 31
modest 27
molasses 92
monkey 112
monster 84
Morocco 97
mortality 99
most 30
motorbike 54
mountain 104
mountainous 104
move 38
muddy 55
mysterious 11